Hume

Currently Available

Dennett
Tadeusz Zawidzki
ISBN 1–85168–484–0

Locke
Edward Feser
ISBN 1–85168–489–1

Nietzsche
Robert Wicks
ISBN 1–85168–485–9

Rawls
Paul Graham
ISBN 1–85168–483–2

Wittgenstein
Avrum Stroll
ISBN 1–85168–486–7

Forthcoming

Aquinas
Edward Feser

Berkeley
Harry M. Bracken

Derrida
David Cunningham

Dewey
David Hildebrand

Dostoevsky
Diane Oenning Thompson

Eco
Florian Mussgnug

Habermas
David Ingram

Hobbes
Alistair Edwards

Huxley
Kieron O'Hara

Irigaray
Rachel Jones

Jung
Susan Rowland

Hume

Harold Noonan

ONEWORLD THINKERS

ONEWORLD

OXFORD

HUME

Published by Oneworld Publications 2007

ISBN-13: 978–1–85168–493–9
ISBN-10: 1–85168–493–X

Typeset by Jayvee, Trivandrum, India
Cover design by Simon McFadden
Printed and bound in India for Imprint Digital

Oneworld Publications
185 Banbury Road
Oxford OX2 7AR
England
www.oneworld-publications.com

Contents

CONTENTS

Preface

In this book I present a study of the most important themes in the work of the great British philosopher David Hume. The exposition largely follows the order in which these themes appear in his first and greatest work, *A Treatise of Human Nature*. Thus, after an introductory chapter outlining the background to Hume's thought and setting him in the context of his time, the second chapter of this volume examines Hume's theory of the mind, as found in Part I of Book I of the *Treatise*. The third chapter is devoted to Hume's discussion of causation, induction and the idea of necessary connection in Part III, the fourth is concerned with Hume's discussion of belief in the external world, in Section 2 of Part IV, the fifth with his discussion of personal identity in Section 6 of Part IV, and the sixth with Hume's theories of the passions and morality in Books II and III of the *Treatise*. Finally, in chapter 7 Hume's views on religion, as contained in the section of the *Enquiry Concerning Human Understanding* entitled 'Of Miracles', which was originally intended for publication in the *Treatise*, and in his posthumously published *Dialogues Concerning Natural Religion* are expounded.

I am grateful to former colleagues at the University of Birmingham and colleagues at the University of

Nottingham for the care with which they have read and commented on drafts of this material.

References have been given in general according to the Harvard referencing system. However, references to Locke's *Essay Concerning Human Understanding* are by book, chapter and section. Other occasional exceptions to the Harvard system are explained in the bibliography.

H. W. N.

Chapter One

Introduction: Hume's life and work

Hume's life and times

David Hume, the great British philosopher, was born in Edinburgh on 26 April 1711, into a family of strict Presbyterian gentry. He was educated at Edinburgh University, where he acquired grounding in the classical authors, logic and metaphysics, natural philosophy, ethics and mathematics.

In his brief autobiography 'My Own Life' (Hume 1993b: 351–6) he describes this period:

> I ... was seized very early with a passion for literature, which has been the ruling passion of my life. ... My studious disposition ... gave my family a notion that the law was a proper profession for me, but I found an insurmountable aversion to everything but the pursuits of philosophy and general learning; and while they fancied I was pouring upon Voet and Vinnius, Cicero and Virgil were the authors I was secretly devouring.

> (Hume 1993b: 351)

In 1729 Hume embarked upon the philosophical study that was to lead to his writing of his first book, *A Treatise of Human Nature: An Attempt to Introduce the Experimental Method of Reasoning into Moral Subjects* (Hume 1978). In his own words he 'entered upon a new scene

1

of Thought' and pursued it with such intensity that it led to a breakdown in his health.

In the hope that a period of alternative employment would enable him to resume his philosophical studies with renewed vigour Hume took up, in 1734, a post as a merchant's clerk in Bristol, but he soon left for France to continue study and writing. There he lived first at Rheims and then at La Fléche, which contained the Jesuit college in which Descartes had been educated. There, by 1737, he completed the *Treatise*.

The *Treatise* was published anonymously, with Books I and II appearing in 1739, and Book III following in 1740 along with an Appendix which contained some corrections to and modifications of his already published material.

Its reception disappointed Hume. It 'fell dead-born from the press', he wrote, rather inaccurately (Hume 1993a: 352). Its largely hostile and uncomprehending reception, on which Hume's anonymous publication of his own Abstract in 1740 had no effect, left Hume permanently regretful of his haste in publishing so young.

In 1741 and 1742 two volumes of Essays, Moral and Political appeared. These met with some success and in 1745 Hume applied unsuccessfully for the chair of Physical and Pneumatical Philosophy at Edinburgh University. His irreligious reputation was the cause of his failure to be appointed, and the controversy caused him to publish another anonymous pamphlet, *A Letter from a Gentleman to his Friend in Edinburgh*, in which he defended himself against this charge.

In 1748 the *Philosophical Essays Concerning Human Understanding*, later called *An Enquiry Concerning the Human Understanding*, appeared under Hume's own name. This was a rewriting of Book I of the *Treatise*, in a more elegant form, with significant omissions, and one significant addition (section X, 'Of Miracles', which probably contained material originally intended for the *Treatise* but excised when Hume thought to gain the recommendation of Bishop Butler).

In 1751 *An Enquiry Concerning the Principles of Morals*, Hume's revision of Book III of the *Treatise*, was published. He also published *Three Essays Moral and Political* (1748) and *Political Discourses* (1752). In 1752 he again failed to secure a university appointment, being rejected for the Chair of Logic at the University of Glasgow. However, he was appointed to the post of keeper of the Advocates' Library, where he remained until 1757, and which provided him with the resources and opportunity to embark on his six-volume *History of England*, published in parts in 1754, 1756, 1759 and 1762. This, above all, established his literary reputation. During this time Hume also wrote the *Dialogues Concerning Natural Religion* (the main target of which was the argument from design for the existence of God), which he did not publish in his lifetime, presumably out of a concern not to add to his irreligious reputation, and the *Natural History of Religion*, which he did publish in 1757, as part of his controversial *Four Dissertations*, though he can hardly have thought its approach would endear him to the religious authorities.

From 1763 to 1766, in Paris, as private secretary to the British ambassador, Hume was lionized by the French literary establishment, was a favourite of the fashionable ladies, and developed friendships with Diderot, D'Alembert, d'Holbach, Helvetius, Buffon and, unfortunately for Hume, Rousseau. On Hume's return to England in 1766 Rousseau, fleeing from persecution in Switzerland, accompanied him. Later Hume was forced to defend himself in print against Rousseau's unjust accusations about their relationship.

After 1767 until his death he corrected his *History* for new editions, and continued to work on his *Dialogues*. His philosophical work was now sufficiently known for him to be abusively attacked by James Beattie, a pupil of Thomas Reid (1710–1796), whose work was successful enough to drive Hume to a public disowning of the *Treatise* as a 'juvenile work', and an insistence that only the *Enquiries* should be regarded as expressing his opinions.

On his deathbed, Hume composed his brief autobiography 'My Own Life', published in 1777. In this, his final word on the matter, he refers to the lack of success of the *Treatise* as 'proceeding more from the manner than the matter' (Hume 1993b: 352).

Hume died in 1776, at peace, and, as he says in his autobiography, 'detached from life', considering that 'a man of sixty five, by dying, cuts off only a few years of infirmities'. His only expressed regret was that he could not now live to enjoy his growing literary fame (Hume 1993b: 356).

Themes and Arguments in Hume's philosophy

The subtitle of the *Treatise of Human Nature* is '*An attempt to introduce the experimental method of reasoning into Moral Subjects*'. In fact, Hume intended a five-volume work, applying the experimental method of reasoning successively to the five 'moral subjects', or aspects of human nature, comprised in the subjects of the understanding, the passions, morals (in the modern narrower sense), politics and criticism. But the work as we have it is in fact divided into three Books, on the understanding, on passions and on morals. Disappointed by the public reception of the *Treatise*, Hume abandoned his original plan, and attempted to gain a literary reputation by other means.

Book I, 'Of the Understanding', is the most difficult and intellectually ambitious of all Hume's writings. It is concerned with the origin of our 'ideas', the material of our thoughts, and the character and limitations of our intellectual activity. It is divided into four Parts.

In Part I Hume introduces the basic vocabulary and principles he will be appealing to throughout the rest of his work. He begins with a terminological innovation, introducing the term 'perception' to denote the basic elements of his system, the items that are 'before the mind' whenever any mental activity is going on. He divides perceptions into 'impressions' (corresponding to feeling or experience) and 'ideas' (corresponding to thinking). He also distinguishes between 'simple' and 'complex' perceptions. With this terminological apparatus Hume then formulates the most fundamental principle of his system, the so-called Copy Principle, the principle that every simple idea must be a copy of, that is, must resemble and be causally derived from, a simple impression. It is this that defines him as an empiricist. A second division within the class of perceptions which Hume draws in Part I is that between perceptions 'of sensation' and perceptions 'of reflection'. This division does not loom large in Part I, but its significance becomes clear in Part III, where it turns out to be a crucial component in Hume's account of the origin of the idea of necessary connection – in fact, the idea of necessary connection turns out to be an idea of reflection. The distinction is also of fundamental importance in Books II and III, whose subject matter, the passions and moral sentiments, are impressions of reflection.

Another division in Part I is that between ideas that are general, or abstract, and those that are particular. This is a division previously made by Hume's empiricist predecessor, John Locke, but Hume rejects Locke's account of abstract ideas and endorses and elaborates instead Bishop Berkeley's, according to which 'all general ideas are nothing but particular ones, annexed to a certain term, which gives them a more extensive signification, and makes them recall upon occasion other individuals, which are similar to them' (1978: 18). Hume ranks Berkeley's theory very highly. Its significance for him is that it turns out that the only way he is able to account for our ideas of space, time, existence and causation is as Berkeleian abstract ideas.

Three other fundamental elements of Hume's philosophy are introduced in Part I. The first is the Separability Principle: 'Whatever objects are different are distinguishable, and whatever objects are distinguishable are separable by the thought and imagination' (Hume 1978: 18).

The second is the Conceivability Principle: 'Whatever is clearly conceiv'd may exist, and whatever is clearly conceiv'd, after any manner, may exist after the same manner' (Hume 1978: 233). Or, more briefly: 'Nothing of which we can form a clear and distinct idea is absurd and impossible' (Hume 1978: 19).

Together these principles imply that if any objects are distinct they can exist separately – either can exist without the other. And it is this consequence Hume appeals to in rejecting the possibility of real connections between distinct existences, which rejection in turn underpins his rejection of necessary connections between causes and effects, his rejection of the notion of substance (except as applicable universally to anything that can be conceived) and his rejection of a simple self distinct from its perceptions. In some commentary (Wright 1983, Strawson 1989) Hume has been described as a 'sceptical realist', whose scepticism is in fact limited to our possession of positively contentful ideas of these things, but who does not deny their existence in the world. This is inconsistent with the role of the Separability Principle (understood as a principle about the distinctness of objects, as opposed to ideas) just outlined (for further discussion see the third chapter of this volume and Bennett 2001).

The final fundamental element of Hume's thought introduced in Part I is his statement of his three principles of the association of ideas: resemblance, contiguity and cause and effect, which, he believes, account for the order in which our ideas follow one another in our minds, and are also involved in the explanation of our coming to have beliefs in matters of fact beyond our memory and senses and in the origin of the problematic ideas already mentioned.

In Part II of Book I Hume attempts to provide an account of the ideas of space and time and also discusses the ideas of existence and external existence.

His account of the ideas of space and time is as abstract ideas, derived from the 'manners of appearance' in which our perceptions array themselves in spatial and temporal relations (Hume 1978: 35). Of these ideas, that of time is of vital importance in Hume's later account of identity as a fiction of the imagination, which in turn is employed both in his account in Part IV of our belief in an external world and in his account of our belief in an enduring self.

The other important discussion in Part II is Hume's account of our ideas of existence and external existence, that is, existence independent of the mind. The former Hume identifies as an abstract idea, so that the idea of existence 'when conjoined with the idea of any object makes no addition to it' (Hume 1978: 67). Hume's account of external existence in Part II anticipates his extended discussion in Part IV, to which he refers the reader. Here, he insists that we can have no idea of anything 'specifically different from' (Hume 1978: 67), that is, wholly unlike, ideas and impressions, and propounds his dictum: 'To hate, to love, to think, to feel, to see, all this is nothing but to perceive' (Hume 1978: 67).

This hints (by the use of the transitive verb 'perceive') at a central feature of his position, namely, his reification of perception.

Part III of Book I, 'Of knowledge and probability', is also of fundamental importance to Hume's philosophy. Its topic is the explanation of our belief in the existence of a world extended beyond our senses and memory. Because of the way he approaches this topic Hume is led into a discussion of the notion of cause and effect and the resultant Humean account of causation has remained a paradigm of philosophical analysis ever since. Its fundamental contention is that though the idea of necessary connection is an essential component of our idea of the cause–effect relation, there is no necessary connection between the things we call causes and effects themselves. The idea of necessary connection is, in fact, copied from a feeling that arises when a transition is made in thought from the idea, or impression, of the cause to the idea of the effect. Our mistaken belief that causes and effects are themselves necessarily connected is a 'fiction of the imagination', which results from the mind's 'propensity to spread itself on external objects' (Hume 1978: 167).

Our belief that every event must have a cause is to be explained similarly, Hume asserts. It is not in fact a necessary truth that every event has a cause.

Part III is also notable for what has traditionally been taken to be the formulation by Hume, in section VI, of what has come to be known as 'the Problem of Induction'. When we infer to the unobserved from the observed, as when we infer from the past to the future, is our procedure rationally justified, in the sense that our beliefs about the observed provide us with evidence for our beliefs about the unobserved? Whether Hume does pose this question in section VI, and, if so, whether he answers it, are questions that have been much debated amongst Hume scholars. The question Hume himself formulates is 'Whether we are determined by reason to make the transition [from an observed cause to its effect], or by a certain association and relation of perceptions?' (Hume 1978: 88–9).

His answer is emphatic:

> Not only our reason fails us in the discovery of the ultimate connection of causes and effects, but even after experience has informed us of their constant conjunction, 'tis impossible for us to satisfy ourselves by our reason, why we should extend that experience beyond those particular instances which have fallen under our observation.

(Hume 1978: 91–2)

The traditional interpretation of this in the mid-twentieth century, originating perhaps with Russell (1912) (see also Flew 1961, Stove 1965, Bennett 1971, Stroud 1977) was that Hume is here expressing scepticism about induction. As Stroud states what he takes to be Hume's conclusion: 'Past and present experiences give us no ... reason at all to believe anything about the unobserved ... As far as the competition for degrees of reasonableness is concerned, all possible beliefs about the unobserved are tied for last place' (Hume 1977: 52–4).

Perhaps the greatest achievement of Hume scholarship since the publication of Stroud's book has been the refutation of this reading of Hume (see Broughton 1983; Beauchamp and Rosenberg 1981; Cannon 1979; Baier 1991; Loeb 1991, 1995a, b, 2002; Garrett 1997, 2005; Owen 1999). It has become clear as a result of the work of the scholars listed, and others, that Hume is no sceptic about induction; indeed throughout his writings, both in Part III of the *Treatise* and elsewhere, he takes it for granted that induction is justified. According to an influential trend in recent scholarship (originating perhaps with Broughton 1983, but developed by Garrett 1997; Owen 1999; Loeb 2002) his target in the crucial section of Part III is rather the view that the transitions we make in inductive reasoning (what he himself calls 'probable argument') are themselves the product of reasoning. His concern is not with the warrant for our inductive practices but with their origin (taking it for granted that inductive reasoning is justified, his enquiry at this point of course assumes that if reason 'determines' us it must do so through the medium of sound argument). However, scholars who agree on this still dispute about the details. In particular, there is dispute about the notion of reason that Hume has in view. Some think that all Hume is arguing is that if 'reason' is interpreted in a narrow, rationalistic way, which conforms to the deductivist assumption that only valid deductive arguments are any good, then reason has nothing to do with our formation of beliefs about the unobserved on the basis of the observed (Broughton 1983; Beauchamp and Rosenberg 1981; Baier 1991). Others (most emphatically Garrett 1997) take him to be arguing that reason, in the more inclusive sense in which Hume himself uses the term, that is, to cover both demonstrative and probable argument, is not the causal source of our inductive inferences.

Accompanying the recognition that Hume is no sceptic about induction another important development in recent scholarship (due particularly to Loeb 1991, 1995a, b, 2002; Garrett 1997) has been the recognition of the significance of the distinction Hume draws (Hume 1978: 117) between two senses of 'imagination': a wide, normatively neutral sense, in which the term is used to designate the faculty by which we form our fainter (non-memory) ideas, and a narrow, disreputable sense according to which the imagination excludes our demonstrative and probable reasonings. Although our probable inferences are activities of the imagination, therefore, this is not inconsistent with their legitimacy, since they are not exercises of the imagination in the narrow sense. However, as Hume proceeds it turns out that much else in our intellectual life is. It is on this basis that Hume is rightly called a sceptic and this development takes place in Part IV, 'Of the sceptical and other systems of philosophy', (anticipated by the discussion of our belief in a 'necessary connexion' between causes and effects in section XIV of Part III, where this belief is ascribed to our narrow imaginative propensity to 'spread our minds on the world').

The first section of Part IV, 'Of scepticism with regard to reason', contains an argument that reason can never give the slightest grounds for belief, because consistently followed it destroys all belief. Only 'trivial qualities' of the (narrow) imagination sustain belief. The second section of Part IV, 'Of scepticism with regard to the senses', contains Hume's discussion of the nature and causes of our belief in an external world. Hume here argues that this belief is a product of the narrow imagination. In section IV he goes on to argue that belief in an external world is opposed by reason, that is, that 'there is a direct and total opposition betwixt those conclusions we draw from cause and effect and those that persuade us of the continued existence of body'. Part IV also contains Hume's discussion 'Of personal identity', in which the object is again to explain, via the mechanism of narrow imagination, our possession of a false natural belief, the belief in the existence of a unitary enduring self.

Not surprisingly, therefore, Hume himself is prepared to say (in the Abstract) 'the philosophy contain'd in this book is very sceptical' (Hume 1978: 657). In the final section of Part IV he attempts to put the scepticism of the *Treatise* into focus and assess the relationship of his philosophy to traditional scepticism. It is notable that Hume here makes no reference to section VI of Part III, but only to section XIV and sections I and IV of Part IV. His general position – that the preceding parts of the *Treatise* show both the irrefutability and practical insignificance of philosophical scepticism – he perhaps expresses best in the Abstract:

> Almost all reasoning is there [in the *Treatise*] reduced to experience and the belief, which attends experience, is explained to be nothing but a peculiar sentiment, or lively conception produced by habit. Nor is this all, when we believe anything of external existence, or suppose an object to exist a moment after it is no longer perceived, this belief is nothing but a sentiment of the same kind. Our author insists upon several other sceptical topics; and upon the whole concludes, that we assent to our faculties, and employ our reasoning only because we cannot help it. Philosophy would render us entirely Pyrrhonian were not nature too strong for it.
>
> (Hume 1978: 657)

However, the cool detachment of this summary gives little indication of the passionate intensity of the final section of Book I. Here Hume, beginning in 'despair', and fancying himself 'some strange uncouth monster, who not being able to mingle and unite in society, has been expelled from all human commerce, and left utterly abandoned and disconsolate' (Hume 1978: 264), eventually arrives at a position he can live with only by resolving to pursue philosophy in a 'careless manner' (Hume 1978: 273), diffident of his philosophical doubts, as well as his philosophical convictions (and only in virtue of this thoroughgoing diffidence justified in pursuing his investigations into the 'science of man' [Hume 1978: xv]), and prepared to regard philosophy as something to be engaged in when the inclination takes him, and to be abandoned without regret, when, and for so long as, his bent of mind turns away from it to the pleasures of everyday life.

Book I of the *Treatise* contains Hume's discussion of ideas. Books II and III go on to discuss impressions of reflection, 'those other impressions ... called secondary and reflective, as arising from the original impressions or from their ideas' (Hume 1978: 276). As for the original impressions, or 'impressions of sensation', the study of these, Hume says, 'belongs more to anatomists and natural philosophers than to moral' (Hume 1978: 8). Thus Hume regards the *Treatise* in its entirety as discussing all the elements of the mental world that are the proper objects of the student of moral philosophy

Book II is concerned with the impressions of reflection Hume calls 'the passions' – our emotions, feelings and motives. Hume's discussion of these prepares the ground for his moral theory in Book III. It does so, first, by introducing the notion of sympathy – a mechanism which converts ideas into impressions and causes our emotional lives to reflect those of others; and, second, by arguing for Hume's famous anti-rationalist thesis, that 'Reason is and ought only to be the slave of the passions' (Hume 1978: 415).

Book III builds on Book II by developing an anti-rationalist theory of morals. 'Morals excite passions, and produce or prevent action. Reason of itself is utterly impotent in this particular. The rules of morality are therefore not conclusions of our reason' (Hume 1978: 457). Consequently, 'vice and virtue are not matters of fact, whose existence we can infer by reason' (Hume 1978: 468). Feelings or sentiments of praise and blame are pains and pleasures – impressions of reflection – produced by the operation of sympathy on observers of the consequences of virtuous or vicious actions. Hence the capacity for moral distinctions is 'founded entirely on the peculiar fabric and constitution of the human species' (Hume 1975: 170).

After the *Treatise*, as we have already noted, Hume restated, and to an extent revised, the matter of Book I in the *Enquiry Concerning Human Understanding*, the first *Enquiry* as it is often called.

Two uncontroversial differences between Book I of the *Treatise* and the first *Enquiry* may be noted. The first is the greater focus on causation as the chief topic in the latter, and the brevity of the discussion of the sceptical arguments of Part IV of the *Treatise*. (The argument of section I of Part IV is dropped completely and the discussion of scepticism with respect to the external world, the topic of sections II and IV of Part I, is reduced to its bare essentials.) This shift in focus is already heralded, however, in the Abstract, which identifies the argument concerning causation as the chief argument of the book. The second evident difference between Book I of the *Treatise* and the first *Enquiry* is the role assigned to the principles of association in the former. These are not repudiated in the *Enquiry*, but Hume's enthusiasm for them is reduced.

Another notable difference between Book I of the *Treatise* and the first *Enquiry* is the omission from the latter of any discussion of personal identity. But this difference is accounted for by the Appendix, in which Hume states himself dissatisfied with his discussion of the topic in Book I, and declares the whole matter 'a labyrinth' (Hume 1978: 633).

In other respects the first *Enquiry* most obviously differs from Book I of the *Treatise* by addition, rather than by omission. In particular, it contains the two sections 'Of Miracles' and 'Of a particular Providence and of a future state'. But the former was probably originally intended for the *Treatise* itself, and the latter contains no change in Hume's philosophical position. What the two sections do is to make quite clear the irreligiosity of Hume's position; no doubt after it had become clear to him that his attempt in the *Treatise* to render his work inoffensive to religious opinion had failed. The argument 'Of a particular Providence and of a future state' is extended and elaborated in the posthumous *Dialogues Concerning Natural Religion* (Hume 1998).

Book III's moral theory is restated in the *Enquiry Concerning the Principles of Morals*, which differs less obviously in content from the corresponding book of the *Treatise* than the first *Enquiry*, though there are differences of emphasis and a notable downplaying of the role of sympathy. Book II is unenthusiastically summarized in Hume's little-read *Dissertation on the Passions*.

Precursors, influences and effects

First among Hume's precursors to be mentioned, of course, must be Locke and Berkeley, his British Empiricist predecessors.

Locke expresses the general position they have in common with Hume, which is the justification of the standard grouping of the three as 'the British Empiricists', in these words in his *Essay Concerning Human Understanding* (Locke 1961):

> Let us then suppose the mind to be, as we say, white paper, void of all characters, without any ideas. How comes it to be furnished? Whence comes it by that vast store which the busy and boundless fancy of man has painted on it with an almost endless variety? Whence has it all the materials of reason and knowledge? To this I answer in one word, from experience.
>
> (*Essay* II, i.2)

Berkeley writes:

> It is evident to anyone who takes a survey of the objects of human knowledge, that they are either ideas actually imprinted on the senses, or else such as are perceived by attending to the passions and operations of the mind, or lastly ideas formed by help of memory and imagination, either compounding, dividing, or barely representing those originally perceived in the aforesaid ways.
>
> (Berkeley 1949: 41)

Hume's Copy Principle is the most succinct statement of this position.

How much more, in the detail of his arguments, Hume owed to the other two is a matter of controversy. Clearly, in his discussion of personal identity, Hume had Locke's ground-breaking account in mind, though how closely his discussion is intended as a response to Locke can be debated. Berkeley's influence on Hume's discussion of abstract ideas has already been noted. The extent of his influence in other areas, Hume's discussions of space and time, and the external world, for example, is more controversial. But Hume's general attitude to Berkeley is made clear in a footnote in the first *Enquiry*:

> most of the writings of that very ingenious author form the best lessons of scepticism, which are to be found either among the ancient or modern philosophers, Bayle not excepted ... [T]hat all his arguments, though otherwise intended, are, in reality, merely sceptical, appears from this, that they admit of no answer and produce no conviction.

> (Hume 1975: 155)

From a self-avowed sceptic, the praise could not be more fulsome.

Another undoubted influence on Hume was Newtonianism. Hume would have encountered Newtonian science at Edinburgh during his university years, and would have had ample opportunity during the period of voracious reading he undertook thereafter to go further into the Newtonian system of ideas. And, in fact, in his *History of England* Hume refers to Newton in the most complimentary terms.

In the *Treatise* itself Hume never refers explicitly to Newton by name, but it is impossible to miss the deliberate allusion in his description of the principles of association of ideas as 'a kind of ATTRACTION, which in the mental world will be found to have as extraordinary effects as in the natural, and to show itself in as many and as various forms' (Hume 1978: 12–13).

The importance of the influence of Francis Hutcheson (1694–1747) on Hume was argued by Norman Kemp Smith in his monumental work *The Philosophy of David Hume* (1941). Kemp Smith maintained that it was Hutcheson's philosophy which opened out to Hume 'the new Scene of Thought' of which he speaks in his letter of 1734 (Kemp Smith 1964: 41–2), and speculated that in the order of composition Books II and III preceded Book I.

Hutcheson was an exponent of a 'moral sense' theory of ethics. He held that there was an inner sense, which enabled us to discern good and evil. This inner sense was a feeling and did not rest on reason: thus our judgements of good and evil are not based on reason, but feeling.

Hume's ethics clearly parallels Hutcheson's and is inspired by it, though there is not total agreement between the two (a significant difference being Hume's employment of the concept of sympathy). What is controversial is the extent of Hutcheson's influence on Book I of the *Treatise*. Kemp Smith's belief in the importance of this influence is part of his account of Hume's philosophy in general, as a form of naturalism, one that involves the thorough subordination of reason to feeling. The justice of this description will be considered later.

Whether or not Hume's philosophy is to be described as naturalism another possibility is to describe it as scepticism; and since this is Hume's own self-description, all that can be in question is the sense in which it is correct.

Here the relationship of Hume to the sceptics of antiquity and to the great French sceptic Pierre Bayle (1647–1706) needs to be considered.

The relationship of Hume's philosophy to ancient scepticism is clearly of significance. Hume refers to two schools of ancient scepticism: the Pyrrhonian and the Academic, rejecting the former and endorsing, in the *Enquiry* (Hume 1975: 61), the latter. The Pyrrhonist movement took its name from Pyrrho of Elis, who was reported to have secured happiness through putting his scepticism into practice. This practical aspect of their scepticism was very important to the Pyrrhonists.

What we know about the Pyrrhonists we know mostly through the writings of a later member of the school, Sextus Empiricus (late second century AD). In his *Outlines of Pyrrhonism* Sextus defines scepticism as:

> an ability, or mental attitude, which opposes appearances to judgements in any way whatsoever, with the result that owing to the equipollence of the objects and the reasons thus opposed, we are brought firstly to a state of mental suspense and next to a state of 'unperturbedness' or quietude.
>
> (Sextus Empiricus 1933–49: PH1 8)

This definition identifies the three elements in Pyrrhonism which are relevant to Hume's understanding of it and his attitude towards it: the opposing of appearances and judgements, the suspension of judgement and the consequent state of tranquillity or unperturbedness.

The Pyrrhonian activity of opposing appearances and judgments, and generally of opposing to every proposition an equal proposition to force a 'dogmatist' to suspend judgement, is illustrated by Sextus in various examples. Its purpose was not to establish any position, but rather to show that no position was more worthy of acceptance than any other and so to create a suspension of judgement.

Suspending judgement for the Pyrrhonists meant living without belief (dogma), but the Pyrrhonist does not deny appearances. As Sextus explains: 'we do not overthrow the affective sense-impressions which induce our assent involuntarily; and these impressions are "the appearances". And when we question whether the underlying object is such as it appears we grant the fact that it appears' (PH1 19).

It is clear that the Pyrrhonists thought themselves entitled, despite suspending judgement, to engage in all the normal activities of life. As Sextus writes: 'Adhering, then, to appearances, we live in accordance with the normal rules of life, undogmatically, seeing that we cannot remain wholly inactive' (PH1 17).

Sextus is here responding to the challenge that a life without belief is unliveable. This objection was the heart of Hume's own rejection of Pyrrhonism: without belief there is no basis for action.

The third notion central to the Pyrrhonist philosophy is that of tranquillity (*ataraxia*). According to Sextus such tranquillity is a consequence of suspension of judgement (*epoche*). This is again a point on which Hume disagrees with the Pyrrhonists. The perplexity resulting from opposing appearance to judgement (or, in Hume, the narrow imagination to reason), he thinks, gives rise not to tranquillity, but to a 'sensible uneasiness' (Hume 1978: 205) from which the mind 'naturally seeks relief' in a rejection of one of the two opposing principles. In the absence of such a resolution the consequence is not tranquillity but 'despair' (Hume 1978: 264).

The other form of ancient scepticism with which Hume was acquainted was Academic scepticism, the form of scepticism to which Cicero (106–43 BC), Hume's favourite ancient author, was most sympathetic. The most important figure in the history of Academic scepticism was Carneades (214–129 BC). The Academic sceptics rejected the possibility of certain knowledge, but their scepticism was not as radical as that of the Pyrrhonists. In practical life Carneades proposed a theory of probability as a guide to life. He distinguished three levels of probability: the probable, the probable and undisputed and the probable, undisputed and tested. According to Cicero these probabilities provide the Academic philosopher 'with a canon of judgement both in the conduct of life and in philosophical investigations and discussion' (Cicero 1933: 509). In Part III of Book I of the *Treatise*, after the arguments about cause and effect which used to be read as the clearest indication of Hume's scepticism, there occur three sections on probability and a section on 'Rules by which to judge of causes and effects', and in the Abstract of the *Treatise* Hume writes:

The celebrated Monsieur Leibnitz has observed it to be a defect in the common systems of logic, that they are very copious when they explain the operations of the understanding in the forming of demonstrations, but are too concise when they treat of probabilities and those other measures of evidence on which life and action entirely depend, and which are our guides even in most of our philosophical speculations ... The author of the *Treatise of*

17

> *Human Nature* seems to have been sensible of this defect in these philosophers, and has endeavoured as much as he can to supply it.
>
> (Hume 1978: 646–7)

The notion of probability is also central to the section 'Of miracles' in the first *Enquiry* and Hume's discussion draws heavily on his treatment of proofs and probabilities in the *Treatise*, which is repeated, more briefly, in the *Enquiry*.

A further important influence on Hume's thought in general, and on his scepticism in particular, was the great French sceptic, Pierre Bayle.

Apart from the general influence exerted by Bayle on his understanding and treatment of scepticism, two places in Book I of the *Treatise* where Bayle's influence is particularly visible are the discussion of space, time and vacuum in Part II, and section V of Part IV in which Hume argues that the hypothesis of an immaterial soul substance is no more intelligible than that of a material soul substance; both are products of narrow imagination.

In the latter discussion Hume uses arguments from the article in Bayle's *Dictionary on Spinoza*, in the course of a teasing comparison which is intended to show that the theologians' 'doctrine of the immateriality, simplicity and indivisibility of a thinking substance is a true atheism, and will serve to justify all those sentiments, for which Spinoza is so universally infamous' (Hume 1978: 240). Perhaps the most significant feature of this argument is the extent to which it reveals Hume's commitment to the reification of perceptions.

Of all the topics discussed in Hume's philosophy perhaps the most important is causation, and in this connection the influence of Nicolas Malebranche (1638–1715) is crucial (for an extended investigation to which the summary below is greatly indebted see McCracken 1983).

In Book I of the *Treatise* Malebranche is mentioned by name only twice: in section XIV of Part III, 'Of the idea of necessary connexion', and in section V of Part IV, 'Of the immateriality of the soul'. But the text to which the former reference is attached provides convincing evidence of the attention with which Hume read

Malebranche. Arguing for his conviction that the power by which a cause produces its effect is perfectly unknowable Hume writes: 'There are some, who maintain, that bodies operate by their substantial form; others by their accidents or qualities; several, by their matter and form: some by their form and accidents, others by certain virtues and faculties distinct from all this' (Hume 1978: 158). Malebranche writes: 'There are philosophers who maintain that second causes act by ... their substantial form. Many by Accidents and Qualities, some by Matter and Form, others by Form and Accidents, others still by certain virtues, or of qualities distinct from all this' (Malebranche 1700: 156, quoted in McCracken 1983: 257).

Malebranche was an Occasionalist. He denied that anything was a true cause except the infinite will of God. Anything else, however constantly conjoined with any other object, is a mere secondary cause or occasion on which the one true cause, divine power, acts to bring about its effect.

The argument that Malebranche gives for this doctrine starts from his definition of a true cause: 'A true cause as I understand it is one such that the mind perceives a necessary connection between it and its effect' (Malebranche 1980: 450, quoted in McCracken 1983: 261). But, Malebranche insists, there is never perceivable such a necessary connection between any two finite beings. Therefore, it is only God who is a true cause since it is a contradiction that He should will and that what He wills should not happen. Thus in the whole of the created world there is no true causal connection.

> We are, of course, disposed to suppose that we can see that this is not the case and that we can see the force in one body communicated to another. But, Malebranche asserts, we are mistaken: Your eyes, in truth, tell you, say, that when a body at rest is struck by another it begins to move. ... But do not judge that bodies have in themselves some moving force, or that they can communicate such a force to other bodies when they strike them, for you see no such thing happen as that.
>
> (Malebranche 1968, vol. 10: 48, quoted in McCracken 1983: 259)

19

The cause of our mistake is that a constant association of two things in our experience so acts on our brains as to create a habit of expectation, so that whenever we see one of the objects we form an expectation of the other; and this habit of expectation, the work of the imagination, we mistake for a necessary connection between the two things. This, according to Malebranche, is why everyone concludes that a moving ball which strikes another is the true cause of the motion it communicates to the other, and that the soul's will is the true cause of movement in the arms – because it always happen that a ball moves when struck by another, and that our arms move almost every time we want them to.

Hume, of course, was no Occasionalist, and made his opposition clear at every opportunity. But even given just this sketchy outline of Malebranche's views we can conclude that the extent of his agreement with Malebranche is considerable: like Malebranche he insists that in defining causation there is a necessary connection to be taken into account, and so rejects any mere regularity analysis of causation of the type that latter day 'Humeans' have put forward: like Malebranche he argues that no necessary connection can be discovered between any two finite things because there is no contradiction given any two distinct things, that one should exist and the other not; like Malebranche he denies that we can ever perceive the operation of any power or productive principle; like Malebranche he thinks, nevertheless, that we universally hold the mistaken belief that such finite items as the movements of two billiard balls are necessarily connected; and, finally, like Malebranche he explains this mistake as resulting merely from the operation of the imagination, acted on by experienced constant conjunctions, which creates a habit of expectation which the mind externalizes as a necessary connection between the constantly conjoined objects. Where Hume parts company with Malebranche is only in denying that his notion of 'true causation' has any applicability, and he does so only because he rejects innate ideas, and, therefore, denies that we have any idea of God's will which can enable us to discover any more of a necessary connection between it and God's actions, than between any finite will and the actions of its possessor. Thus he writes in the context of his discussion of the idea of necessary connection:

> The principle of innate ideas being allowed to be false, it follows that the supposition of a deity can serve us in no stead, in accounting for that idea of agency, which we search for in vain in all the objects, which are presented to our senses, or which we are internally conscious of in our own minds. For if every idea be derived from an impression, the idea of a deity precedes from the same origin; and if no impression, either of sensation or reflection, implies any force or efficacy, 'tis equally impossible to discover or even imagine any such active principle in the deity.

(Hume 1978: 160)

Finally, in looking at influences on Hume's thought, we should not ignore Descartes (1596–1650). The indirect influence of Descartes on Hume, through Malebranche, one of his followers, is undeniable, as we have just seen, but the extent of Descartes' influence is far greater than this indicates. As Thomas Reid (1941) wrote, Hume shared, along with Malebranche, Locke and Berkeley, a common 'system of the understanding' which 'may still be called the Cartesian system'.

The one great point of similarity between all these philosophers is their conception of philosophy as beginning with epistemology, the theory of knowledge. For all of them the primary question the philosopher must answer concerns the nature and limits of human knowledge. This conception of philosophy is the viewpoint that defines what the textbooks call 'Modern Philosophy'. Descartes, unlike earlier philosophers, asked not just what the world is like, but how we can know what it is like. He thought also that he had provided an account of how this question could be answered, by starting from the one immediate, indubitable datum of consciousness he identified by the Method of Doubt, the Cogito, 'I think therefore I am', and 'working out' to an external world, via indubitable principles of inference (such as that the cause of an effect must have at least as much reality as the effect). His successors, however, found his appeal to such principles unconvincing and thus were left to confront the epistemological problem for themselves.

Hume refers to the Method of Doubt as a species of antecedent scepticism, scepticism antecedent to all study and philosophy, and explains his rejection of it in the first *Enquiry*. Such antecedent scepticism,

> Inculcated by Des Cartes and others as a sovereign preservative against error and precipitate judgement [he says] recommends an universal doubt, not only of all our former opinions and principles, but also of our very faculties; of whose veracity, say they, we must assure ourselves, by a chain of reasoning, deduced from some original principle, which cannot possibly be fallacious or deceitful.

But, he goes on,

> Neither is there any such original principle ... above all others that are self-evident and convincing: Or if there were, could we advance a step beyond it, but by the use of those very faculties, of which we are supposed to be already diffident. The Cartesian doubt, therefore, were it ever possible to be attained by any human creature (as it plainly is not), would be entirely incurable; and no reasoning could ever bring us to a state of assurance and conviction on any subject.
>
> (Hume 1975: 149–50)

Another point of difference between Descartes and Hume lies in their metaphysics. Descartes maintained that the mind was an immaterial substance 'really distinct' from and independent of body and the notion of substance here is a fundamental concept for Descartes, as it is for his Rationalist successors Leibniz (1646–1716) and Spinoza (1632–1677). Hume decisively rejects it, and with it dualism in the Cartesian form. For the notion of 'substance', as independent existence, he claims, applies to everything that can be conceived, since there are no real connections and everything is, therefore, 'really distinct', in Descartes' sense, from everything else. 'Substance' is, therefore, at least an empty term (and consequently of no use to anyone), and possibly a meaningless one. The mind, in particular, is not an immaterial substance, but a 'bundle of perceptions' and the Cartesian 'I' is a fiction. Thus, whether or not Hume's basic principles are Cartesian, the position he finally arrives at could not be more radically opposed to that of Descartes. His position is, in fact, the final stage in the development of empiricist thought about substance, beginning with Locke's uneasiness with the notion of an unobservable 'something, we know not what' underlying the observable qualities in things, followed by Berkeley's emphatic rejection of the notion of material substance and his attempted accommodation of the concept of the substantial self under the guise of a 'notion' rather than an idea. In this respect Hume's position marks the final emancipation of modern philosophy from that dependence on the Aristotelian and scholastic sources on which Descartes' philosophy was perceived by his successors to rest so unconvincingly.

Finally, a third point of contrast between Descartes and Hume in respect of their attitudes to non-human animals should be noted. Descartes notoriously held that non-human minds were merely automata, without souls, whose behaviour could be given a purely naturalistic, even mechanistic explanation. Man, on the other hand, could never be completely part of the natural world because he possessed free will and reason. Hume, by contrast, insists that all human life is naturalistically explicable, and insists that we can speak as legitimately of the 'reason' of animals as we can of that of man. 'No truth appears to me more evident than that beasts are endowed with thought and reason as much as men' (Hume 1978: 176). In both the *Treatise* and the first *Enquiry* he has a section entitled 'Of the Reason of Animals', and in both he insists on a

> touchstone, by which we may try every system in this species of philosophy: when any hypothesis, therefore, is advanced to explain a mental operation, which is common to men and beasts, we must apply the same hypothesis to both; and as every true hypothesis will abide this trial, so I venture to affirm, that no false one will be ever able to endure it.
>
> (Hume 1978: 177)

His 'own system concerning the nature of the understanding', he argues, receives an 'invincible proof' when put to this test, for though it is sufficiently evident when applied to man, 'with respect to beasts there cannot be the least suspicion of mistake' (Hume 1978: 178).

So far in this section we have been looking at the relation of Hume to his predecessors, but in order to appreciate fully Hume's philosophical importance we need also to attend to his relation to his successors. In Britain Hume's philosophy attracted, as well as a great deal of abuse, the respectful attention of Thomas Reid, and his moral philosophy, specifically, inspired the utilitarianism of Bentham and Mill, and in the twentieth century the emotivism of the Logical Positivists. But by far the most important effect of it was, as he himself put it, to wake Imanuel Kant from his 'dogmatic slumber' (Kant 1977: 5) and to stimulate him to write his *Critique of Pure Reason*. In Kant's view, 'since the origin of metaphysics so far as we know its history, nothing has ever happened which could have been more decisive to its fate than the attack made upon it by David Hume' (Kant 1977: 3).

The particular stimulus to Kant's awakening was Hume's treatment of causation and his denial of any necessary connection between cause and effect. Kant describes Hume's achievement as follows:

> He challenged reason, which pretends to have given birth to this concept of himself, to answer him by what right she thinks anything could be so constituted that if that theory be posited, something else must necessarily be posited, for this is the meaning of the concept, of course. He demonstrated irrefutably that it was entirely impossible for reason to think a priori and by reason of concepts such a conbination as involves necessity. ... Hence he inferred that reason was altogether deluded with reference to this concept.
>
> (Kant 1977: 3)

Kant thought that Hume was right to think that knowledge of particular causal connections could not be known a priori, that is, could only be discovered in experience. However, he thought that Hume went wrong in supposing that this was true also of the general causal maxim that everything has some cause. In Kant's view this was a necessary truth, knowable a priori. Nonetheless, Kant accepted Hume's view that the causal maxim was not something whose denial was so self-contradictory; he insisted that it was not true simply in virtue of conceptual relationships, or the meanings of words, and so was, in the now current terminology he introduced, a 'synthetic' rather than an 'analytic' truth. Hence, he claimed, the causal principle was a 'synthetic a priori' truth. And, as such, Kant thought, it was representative of all metaphysics. For metaphysics properly so-called, consists, he thought, of nothing but a priori synthetic principles and so the possibility of metaphysics becomes the question: 'How are a priori synthetic propositions possible?' (Kant 1977: 21).

Kant's *Critique of Pure Reason* is devoted to answering the question of the possibility of metaphysics framed in this way, and is a work aptly described by a modern commentator as 'of an intellectual depth and grandeur that defy description' (Scruton 1995: 134).

So long as Kant was thought to have 'answered Hume', Hume's philosophy, despite its historical influence, could be thought of as superseded. But in the twentieth century the Logical Positivists (most importantly Carnap, Schlick and Ayer), partly under the influence of Ernst Mach, rejected the Kantian philosophy of the synthetic a priori and reasserted Hume's empiricism. They took as the guiding principle of their philosophy the famous concluding paragraph of Hume's *Enquiry*:

> When we run over our libraries persuaded of these principles, what havoc must we make? If we take in our own hand any volume – of divinity, or school metaphysics, for example – let us ask, 'Does it contain any abstract reasoning concerning quantity or number?' No. 'Does it contain any experimental reasoning concerning matter of fact and existence?' No. Commit it then to the flames, for it can contain nothing but sophistry and illusion.

> (Hume 1975: 165)

Where they had advanced on Hume, they thought, was only in being able to marry his empiricism with the powerful new logic of Frege and Russell.

Thus, Hume is a figure of undeniable importance. Whether right or wrong, his influence brought about, through Kant, a revolution in the way philosophy was conceived (what Kant, in fact, called a 'Copernican revolution') and both his general approach and particular doctrines are still relevant to present-day philosophical debate.

Hume's theory of the mind

Chapter Two

The contents of the mind

In Part I of Book I of the *Treatise* and in sections II and III of the first *Enquiry* Hume presents his theory of ideas, his account of the nature and origin of thought. Taken largely from Locke, to a philosophically informed modern reader it is obscure, since the concept of an 'idea' that he employs seems, in the light of subsequent philosophy, particularly Wittgenstein's, to be deeply problematic.

But to understand the defects of the theory of ideas we must first understand the theory, and to do that we must begin where Hume began, with Locke.

Locke defines an 'Idea' as 'Whatsoever the Mind perceives in itself, ... the immediate object of Perception, Thought or Understanding' (Locke 1961, *Essay* II, viii.8: all subsequent references to *Essay* refer to this volume). According to Locke, whenever mental activity takes place ideas are 'before the mind' as the 'direct objects' of the mind's awareness. This is so whenever we exercise any of our five senses, feel any sensation, or think any thought.

It is natural to protest that Locke is ignoring a huge difference, the difference between perception and thought. What could be more different than *the sensory experience of seeing a tree*, and *the thought of a tree*, had

27

perhaps with one's eyes closed, or in the dark? A modern philosopher is tempted to insist on an ambiguity: 'idea' means either 'content of a sensory experience' or 'exercise of a concept in thought'. It cannot mean both.

However, in Locke it *does* mean both, for Locke's account *assimilates* thought to perception, that is, it treats thinking as a transaction with materials of the same kind as are involved in perception. This is because Locke's intention is to explain not only what thought is, but also its origin, and via the assimilation of thought and perception he can give a simple account: *all* thought is derived from experience.

But there are two types of experience – outer and inner – and two types of ideas: *ideas of sensation*, which come into our mind via our senses, and *ideas of reflection*, the mind's representations of its own activities. Examples of the former are: 'Those ideas we have of *yellow, white, heat, cold, soft, hard, bitter, sweet*, and all those which we call sensible qualities' (*Essay* II, i.3). Examples of the latter are: '*perception, thinking, doubting, believing, reasoning, knowing, willing*, and all the different workings of our own minds' (*Essay* II, i.3).

So Locke's fuller answer to the question 'Whence has [the mind] all the materials of reason and knowledge?' is: 'Our observation employed either about external sensible objects or about the internal operations of our minds perceived and reflected on by ourselves, is that which supplies our understandings with the materials of thinking' (*Essay* II, i.2).

Locke's theory, then, has two elements: (i) an account of mental activity that assimilates perception and thought and (ii) an account of the origin of thought that *limits* the thinkable to the experienced or experienceable.

To defend the second component of this theory Locke needs another division within ideas, namely, the division between *simple* and *complex* ideas. Simple ideas are those 'in the reception of which the mind is only passive' and are 'received from sensation and reflection' (*Essay* II xix.1). The mind then performs various operations on these simple ideas, which result in complex ideas. Thus, Locke claims, the mind can generate all the materials of thought from those received through sensation and reflection: 'by repeating and joining *ideas* that it had either from objects of sense or from its own operations about them' (*Essay* II, xii.8). Since to think is to operate with ideas it follows that 'the simple *ideas* we receive from sensation and reflection are the boundaries of our thoughts' (*Essay* II, xxii.29). Since we cannot know what we cannot think, they are also the boundaries of our knowledge.

In all this Hume follows Locke, with some modifications. He calls the 'objects of the mind' not 'ideas' but 'perceptions', distinguishing 'perceptions' into 'ideas' and 'impressions', noting that in doing so he is 'restoring the [former] word to its original sense, from which Mr Locke had perverted it' (Hume 1978: 2), and 'employing [the latter] in a sense somewhat different from the usual' (Hume 1975: 18). Like Locke he distinguishes between perceptions of sensation and perceptions of reflection. Thus he makes a fourfold division between (i) impressions of sensation (seeing a colour or feeling a pain), (ii) impressions of reflection (feeling fear), (iii) ideas of sensation (the thought of a colour or pain) and (iv) ideas of reflection (the thought of fear). These enter the mind, according to Hume, in the order (i), (iii), (ii) and (iv). Again, like Locke, Hume distinguishes between simple and complex ideas, and adheres to the fundamental empiricist thesis that all knowledge derives from experience. But Hume does not recognize every idea-forming operation that Locke acknowledges, and, in particular, as we shall see, not the operation of abstraction. Also Hume does not accept the possibility of any necessary connection between simple ideas, whereas Locke does (*Essay* II, vii, 7) and so some ideas that are simple for Locke (*Essay* II, iii–vii), extension and space, for example, are complex for Hume.

Hume and Locke may be compared with respect to two other points: the *ontological status* of ideas, and their *representational quality*.

Often Locke speaks of ideas as entities. The impression given is that ideas are independently existing *things* with qualities of their own, rather than mere states or properties of persons whose existence consists merely in their thinking or perceiving in certain ways. If so we can enquire (i) what qualities our ideas have in themselves, independently of the relations they stand in to other things or to us, (ii) what relation we stand in to our ideas, and (iii) what relations our ideas stand in to the things – the trees and dogs and houses and people – we think of ourselves as encountering in our everyday perceptual transactions.

It is controversial whether Locke is to be thought of as thus 'reifying' ideas. According to one interpretation of Locke's theory of perception, for a man to see a tree involves three things standing in suitable relations: a man, an idea of a tree and a tree. The man sees the tree if and only if he perceives the idea, which is caused by and resembles (in certain respects) the tree. Thus our relationship to the things we ordinarily take ourselves to perceive is mediated by ideas which form a kind of veil between the external world and us. On an alternative account this is a mistaken interpretation. Thus John Yolton writes: 'The way of ideas is Locke's method of recognising mental features of seeing. It does not place the perceiver in some vale [sic] of ideas forever trying to break out into the world of physical objects' (Yolton 1970: 132).

According to this latter account a person's 'perceiving an idea' is, for Locke, no more a genuine relation between the person and the idea than a person's being 'in' a mood is a genuine relation between the person and the mood (see Bennett 1971: 31–5 for the development of this analogy). Moods are non-relational states *of* people. A mood exists just if a person is 'in' it. Moods are *adjectival* on people: anything that can be sensibly said about moods can be paraphrased in a clearly non-relational formulation. Thus, for a person to be in a happy mood is for a person to be happy, for a person to be in a sad mood is for that person to be sad, for a person to be in a short-lived happy mood is for that person to be briefly happy, and so on. The same is true, *mutatis mutandis*, of Lockean ideas on the alternative interpretation. A person's having an idea is a non-relational state. For an idea to exist is just for a person to 'have' it. Ideas are adjectival on people.

It is unclear which of these two interpretations of Locke's theory of ideas is correct. Hume's position, by contrast, is completely unambiguous. Hume reifies perceptions. He regards all perceptions as things, indeed as substances, in so far as that

notion makes any sense, and the relation betwee
and perception – that of perceiving – as a genuine rel;
between independently existing things (Hume 197
he accepts that perceptions are not adjectival on perceiv....
it makes sense to suppose that perceptions can exist independently of being perceived and that for a person to be in any psychological state is for a certain relational statement to be true of that person.

Or rather, this is the position from which Hume starts, but once perceptions are considered as ontologically on a par with perceivers it is a short step to the conclusion that there is no perceiver apart from perceptions, so that there is, after all, no genuine relation of perceiving between perceiver and perception qua two independent things. Not, however, because perceptions are adjectival on perceivers, but rather because perceivers are *themselves* ontologically constituted out of perceptions – are 'bundles' of perceptions, as Hume puts it. As we shall see later it is this line of thought that leads Hume to his conception of the self as a fiction.

The second point of difference between Locke and Hume mentioned above concerns the representational quality of ideas/perceptions (see also Norton 1993: 30).

According to the Lockean account we can perceive and think of things other than ideas because our ideas represent them. How we can know that there is anything ideas represent is indeed a large problem for Locke – it is the problem of our knowledge of the external world. Nevertheless, Locke does think that we can be justified in thinking that there is an external world and that our ideas represent it.

Ideas represent in two ways. Some represent via resemblance, as a painting of a cat represents a cat because the images and colours on the canvas bear a resemblance to those of a cat. Thus, Locke claims, the ideas of 'solidity, extension, figure, motion or rest and number' (*Essay* II, viii.9) 'are *resemblances* of [these qualities], and their patterns do really exist in the bodies themselves' (*Essay* II, viii.15–18).

However, other ideas do not resemble anything in the material world. Ideas of colours, tastes, smells etc., do not resemble their ᴊuses in the objects perceived. Rather their causes are powers to produce the appropriate ideas. Thus in the case of these ideas representation is not via resemblance. Rather it is by causation:

> [T]hough whiteness and coldness are no more in snow than pain is, yet those ideas ... being in us the effects of powers in things without us ... are real *ideas* in us whereby we distinguish the qualities ... in things themselves. ... These ... appearances being designed to be the marks whereby we are to know and distinguish things which we have to do with, our *ideas* do as well serve to that purpose and are as real distinguishing characters, whether they be only constant effects or exact resemblances of something in the things themselves.

> (*Essay* II, xxx.2)

The distinction between ideas that represent by resembling and those that represent by causation is the distinction between ideas of primary qualities and ideas of secondary qualities. This distinction makes it difficult for Locke to give an account of how ideas represent, and he offers a bifurcated account to accommodate the complexities the primary/secondary distinction brings with it.

Hume does not. He takes it to be a consequence of 'the modern philosophy', i.e. Locke's philosophy, that the whole notion of perceptions representing external things must be abandoned. For, he thinks, it is 'universally allowed by modern enquirers' (Hume 1975: 154) and susceptible to a proof which is 'as satisfactory as can possibly be imagined' (Hume 1978: 228) that all the sensible qualities of objects, colours, sounds, tastes, smells, heat and cold, 'Exist not in the objects themselves, but are perceptions of the mind without any external archetype or model, which they represent' (Hume 1975: 154).

But 'If this be allowed with regard to secondary qualities, it must also follow with regard to the supposed primary qualities of extension and solidity' (Hume 1975: 154).

The idea of extension is entirely derived from the senses of sight and feeling, so if all qualities perceived by the senses are in the mind, the same must be true of extension (Hume 1975: 154): 'An extension, that is neither tangible nor visible, cannot possibly be conceived: and a tangible or visible extension, which is neither hard nor soft, black nor white is equally beyond the reach of human conception' (Hume 1975: 155).

Thus, Hume concludes, the opinion of external existence is 'contrary to reason: at least, if it be a principle of reason that all sensible qualities are in the mind, not in the object' (Hume 1975: 155). Or as he puts it in the *Treatise*, when we reason from cause and effect, as the modern philosophers do, the conclusion is 'that neither colour, sound, taste nor smell have a continu'd and independent existence' and 'when we exclude these sensible qualities there is nothing in the universe which has such an existence' (Hume 1978: 231).

Hume consequently wholly rejects the Lockean picture of a world of external objects, possessing primary but no secondary qualities. Within his classificatory scheme ideas represent, and causally derive from, impressions, but impressions represent nothing. In particular this is so of impressions of sensation 'which arise from the soul originally, from unknown causes' (Hume 1978: 7) – a comment from the beginning of the *Treatise* whose significance only emerges two hundred and twenty pages later, in the section 'Of the modern philosophy'.

Impressions and ideas

For Hume, then, his subject matter, as a moral philosopher, can only be our perceptions, qua perceptions, and the first distinction Hume makes within these, from which everything else stems, is the division between impressions and ideas. This distinction, Hume says, corresponds to the distinction between *feeling* and *thinking*. ('Feeling' here refers to any sense-experience, feelings of pain and pleasure, and passions and emotions.) But Hume also characterizes it as a distinction between those perceptions 'which enter with most force and violence into the soul' and 'the faint images of these in thinking and reasoning'.

> By the term *impression,* then, I mean all our more lively percep-
> tions, when we hear, or see, or feel, or love, or hate, or desire, or will
> ... ideas ... are the less lively perceptions, of which we are conscious,
> when we reflect on any of those sensations.

(Hume 1975: 18)

Thus the difference between impressions and ideas for Hume is merely a difference in degree: a difference between *lively, vivid,* or *forceful* perceptions and those that are fainter, less lively, vivid or forceful. That is to say, for Hume there is no difference of kind between what 'passes before the mind' when one sees a tree and when one thinks of a tree. This is explained within Hume's theory of mind by his thesis that ideas are faint *images* of impressions. Just as one can see a tree so one can imagine, picture, a tree. Just as one can hear a tune played on a piano so one can imagine, or play through, the tune in one's mind. Now it seems that there is some-thing in common between what occurs in the former situation in each case, and what occurs in the latter situation. What is going on in the one situation is like, though different from, what is going on in the other situation. Hume attempts to capture the difference using the vocabulary of 'liveliness' or 'vividness' or 'vivacity' or 'forcefulness', but he does not think that he is thereby *explaining* the difference. Rather he takes it to be a difference with which everyone is acquainted (Hume 1978: 1) which it 'requires no nice discernment or metaphysical head to mark' (Hume 1975: 18).

However, if the difference between seeing a tree and forming an image of a tree *can* be characterized in this way, then the same must be true of the difference between seeing a tree and thinking of a tree *if thinking of something is merely to have an image of it in mind.* But this imagist theory of thought *is* Hume's theory of thought. Hence he can think that sensory perception and thinking differ only in being transactions with entities – impressions in the one case and ideas in the other – which themselves differ only in respect of degree of a quality appropriately called 'vivacity', 'vivid-ness', 'liveliness' or 'forcefulness'.

The notion of vivacity is a metaphor Hume never cashes, but it has two features important to him. First, that differences in degree of vivacity are always phenomenological. Impressions and ideas *appear* different and do not differ merely in their relations to other things, and in particular, not merely in their causal origin. 'The most lively thought is inferior to the dullest sensation' (Hume 1975: 17). Hume acknowledges that occasionally 'they may very nearly approach to each other' (Hume 1978: 2), but, 'except the mind be disordered by disease or madness', ideas can never 'arrive at such a pitch of vivacity, as to render these perceptions altogether indistinguishable' (Hume 1975: 17) from impressions. The second feature of vivacity important to Hume is that it is the very same quality that, by differing in degree, distinguishes belief from mere thought. This has to be so because his only account of belief is 'a lively (or vivacious) idea associated with a present impression', and his only explanation of how belief comes about is that vivacity is transmitted from an impression to an associated idea. Thus Hume's explanation of the phenomenon of belief comes to nothing unless the *same* notion of vivacity can be applied to impressions and thoughts.

The Copy Principle and the missing shade of blue

For Hume ideas are copies of impressions: they do not merely resemble impressions; they are causally derived from them as photographs from their originals.

Hume represents this thesis as an empirical discovery. He first notices that on a quick survey it looks as if 'all the perceptions of the mind are double and appear both as impressions and ideas. Ideas and impressions appear always to correspond to each other' (Hume 1978: 3), but he then notes that 'Many of our complex ideas never had impressions, that corresponded to them. ... I can imagine to myself such a city as the New Jerusalem ... tho' I never saw any such' (Hume 1978: 3). 'What never was seen, or heard of, may yet be conceived; nor is any thing beyond the power of thought, except what implies an absolute contradiction' (Hume 1975: 18).

Hume concludes '... the rule is not universally true' that there is an exact correspondence between *complex* impressions and ideas, but 'every simple idea has a simple impression, which resembles it; and every simple impression a correspondent idea' (Hume 1978: 3).

Moreover, 'when we analyze our thoughts and ideas ... we always find that they resolve themselves into such simple ideas as were copied from a precedent feeling or sentiment' (Hume 1975: 19). 'We may prosecute this enquiry to what length we please; where we shall always find, that every idea which we examine is copied from a similar impression' (Hume 1975: 19).

Thus Hume establishes the Copy Principle on the basis of observation, as a matter of fact discovery. So when he immediately goes on to note that there is one 'contradictory phenomenon' which may prove that 'it is not absolutely impossible for ideas to arise, independent of their correspondent impressions' (Hume 1975: 20), he means more than that it is *conceivable* that this should happen. Rather, he means that it is in some sense an epistemic possibility, which we can have no reason to believe does not actually occur.

The 'one contradictory phenomenon' is the notorious shade of blue. Consider some particular shade of blue, and imagine a man who has, as it happens, experienced all other shades of blue except this one. Could he not supply it from his imagination, by arraying all the other shades of blue in a sequence and observing the gap in the spectrum where the missing shade would be? Yet the idea of the missing shade of blue, Hume insists, is a simple idea. So in this case, he claims, we can form a simple idea without any corresponding simple impression – and, we may add, he does not think that this is a mere possibility, on a par with the sun's falling out of the sky, but something that, for all we know, actually occurs. Yet he is remarkably complacent: 'this instance is so singular, that it is scarcely worth our observing, and does not merit that for it alone we should alter our general maxim' (Hume 1975: 21).

Commentators have found this attitude extremely puzzling, given the polemical manner in which Hume appeals to the Copy Principle to question the significance of philosophical notions like substance and necessary connection. For if, in fact, there *can* be, and for all anyone knows, *are*, simple ideas not preceded by corresponding simple impressions, how can Hume argue that a particular philosophical notion is bogus because there is no impression from which it is derived?

The Copy Principle and empiricism

To explore this question further first note a further point about Hume's distinction between impressions and ideas. (Here I am greatly indebted to Bennett 1971, chapter IX.) His 'official' view is that (i) impressions and ideas differ only in their degrees of forcefulness and vivacity and (ii) this difference corresponds to the difference between feeling and thinking. But he has a tendency, inconsistent with this, to equate impressions with the objects of veridical perception.

This surfaces, for example, in his remark in the *Treatise* that 'in a sleep, in a fever, in madness or in any very violent emotion of the soul, our ideas may approach to our impressions' (Hume 1978: 1–2), and in his statement in the *Enquiry* that '*except* the mind be disordered by disease or madness' (my emphasis) ideas are never altogether indistinguishable from impressions (Hume 1975: 16).

If in sleep, fever or madness, *impressions* are before the mind, there is no difficulty here, and Hume's official way of distinguishing ideas from impressions gives him no reason not to say this. However, if impressions occur only in *veridical* perception the non-veridical states involved in sleep, fever or madness cannot be impressions. Thus Hume's refusal to take what is, given his 'official' view, the easy way out of the difficulty he here confronts is some evidence for his tendency to equate impressions with veridical sensory states.

Now note another point. Hume holds that ideas are the constituents of thoughts, i.e., are concepts. But a term has meaning only if it expresses a concept. So Hume's account of *thought* doubles as an account of *linguistic understanding* and his account of the origin of ideas can be understood as a thesis about the preconditions of understanding – the thesis of *meaning empiricism*.

Putting these points together we can understand Hume's Copy Principle as entailing the thesis (A): A simple (indefinable) general term can be understood only if something that falls under it has been encountered in veridical sensory experience.

It is clear that Hume does take (A) to be part of his position. One piece of evidence for this is his contention, in confirmation of the Copy Principle, that 'If it happen, from a defect of the organ, that a man is not susceptible of any species of sensation, we always find that he is as little susceptible of the correspondent ideas' (Hume 1975: 20).

In general, unless we understand the Copy Principle as involving something like thesis (A) it is impossible to see how the evidence he cites for it is relevant.

(A) is still a *genetic* thesis about the past causes of present understanding. However, a possible resolution of the puzzle of the missing shade of blue may now be approached by noting, with Bennett, that meaning empiricism need not take the form of a genetic thesis. Its heart is the thought that experience *in some way* sets limits to what is expressible in language. In Hume and Locke this thought takes the form of a genetic thesis: one can only express in language those features of the world of which *one has had* experience (or which one can construct out of those features of which one has had experience). But an alternative non-genetic formulation is that one can only express in language features of the world that *are capable of being encountered in* experience.

The case of the missing shade of blue is no counter-example to this formulation. For there is no suggestion that the missing shade of blue is *unencounterable*. By contrast, Hume could not allow that an impression of substance or necessary connection in the world is simply something that has, as a matter of fact, not been encountered by anyone. Impressions corresponding to these concepts, Hume thinks, are *impossible*.

Thus, Bennett suggests, if we suppose that, at some level of his thought, Hume recognized that what really mattered to him was merely this non-genetic form of meaning empiricism, we can understand why he is unperturbed by the case of the missing shade of blue, and thinks his polemical deployment of the Copy Principle justified despite it. This is one suggestion about how to resolve the puzzle of Hume's insouciance concerning the missing shade of blue. I now turn to a second, which again crucially involves the thought that what is really important to Hume is a weaker form of empiricism than that he officially espouses. (For a fuller exposition of this solution see Fogelin 1992.)

The first point to be noted here is, as Fogelin expresses it, that there is a kind of atomism which Hume does *not* accept, namely that 'each simple impression [or simple idea] is a pure content standing in no systematic relationship to any other simple impression [or idea] except for being qualitatively identical with it or simply qualitatively different from it' (Fogelin 1992: 72). Thus only complex impressions can bear relations of similarity or dissimilarity to one another that do not reduce simply to identity or difference. In particular, only complex impressions can resemble one another to various degrees (in virtue of sharing more or fewer parts).

Hume explicitly denies this in the Appendix to the *Treatise*:

Even different simple ideas may have similarity or resemblance to each other; nor is it necessary that the point ... of resemblance ... be distinct and separable from that in which they differ. *Blue* and *green* are different simple ideas, but are more resembling than *blue* and *scarlet*; tho' their perfect simplicity excludes all possibility of separation or distinction. ... of this we may be certain, even from the very abstract terms *simple idea*. They comprehend all simple ideas under them. These resemble each other in their simplicity. And yet from their very nature ... this circumstance, in which they resemble, is not distinguishable nor separable from the rest. 'Tis the same case with all the degrees in any quality.

(Hume 1978: 637)

It is this way of thinking of simple ideas and impressions that leads Hume to his example of the missing shade of blue. The various shades of blue, although simple, can be arrayed in sequence with the most closely resembling shades being placed together. Then, in such a linear arrangement, if one shade of blue is missing there will be a noticeable gap – a place where two adjacent shades are noticeably less resembling than the other adjacent shades. In this circumstance, Hume thinks, the mind will be able to make for itself the simple idea out of the materials already presented to it.

This is very different from the situation Hume has in mind when he denies, immediately before introducing the example of the missing shade of blue, that a Laplander has any notion of the relish of wine (Hume 1975: 20). Perhaps a Laplander could acquire such a notion if he were presented with a sequence of more and less resembling tastes, so arranged as to indicate, as in the case of the shades of blue, the absence of one particular taste. But Hume clearly does not have any such situation in mind. Rather, he introduces the example simply to indicate that simple impressions of a particular sense may be unavailable to a perceiver not only when his organs are defective, but also when they have never been activated to produce a particular impression (Hume 1975: 20).

The shade of blue thus *is* a counter-example to the Copy Principle, just as Hume says. But it is not a counter-example to a slightly weaker principle that can be stated as follows: (B) Any simple idea is (a) a copy of a simple resembling impression or (b) an idea of the degree of a particular quality produced in the mind by the presentation thereto of simple impressions of contiguous degrees of the quality.

Although this principle is weaker than the Copy Principle it still requires simple ideas to be preceded in the mind by simple impressions related to them in a certain way: just not by exact resemblance. Thus admitting the missing shade of blue as a counter-example to the Copy Principle need not be seen as the total rejection of empiricism it might at first seem. But can Hume's polemical use of the Copy Principle be understood if we take this weaker form of empiricism, represented by principle (B), to be the only form to which he is truly committed? It can. The philosophical concepts Hume attacks using the Copy Principle – concepts like substance and necessary connection in the world – are not concepts like that of the missing shade of blue. They are not concepts of degrees of a quality. Perhaps it makes sense to speak of 'degrees of substantiality'. But the concept of substance is not itself the concept of a determinate degree of some determinable quality. The same holds of the concept of necessary connection.

Thus the exception to the Copy Principle provided by the missing shade of blue can be explained in a way that does not extend to these problematic philosophical concepts, and so Hume's confidence that the unqualified Copy Principle can be applied to them is justifiably undiminished by it.

The association of ideas

According to Hume, once ideas are derived from impressions, their occurrence in the mind exhibits regularities that can be reduced to three general patterns. These patterns – the principles of the association of ideas – are: *resemblance, contiguity in time and place* and *cause and effect*.

Thus 'A picture naturally lead our thoughts to the original: the mention of one apartment in a building naturally introduces an enquiry or discourse concerning others: and if we think of a wound, we can scarcely forbear reflecting on the pain which follows it' (Hume 1975: 24).

It is implausible that every transition in thought can be explained by appeal to just these three relations, and Hume's sensitivity to this possible objection is shown by his stress in the *Treatise* on 'the full extent of these relations' (Hume 1978: 11). Objects are connected together in the imagination, he says, not only where they are *immediately* resembling, contiguous or causally related, 'but also when there is interposed betwixt them a third object, which bears to both of them any of these relations' (Hume 1978: 11).

Hence Hume shows that it is not actually the three relations he specifies which are for him the principles of association of ideas, but rather, to use a modern technical term, their *ancestrals*: the relations linking any two things between which intermediates can be found linked by the three specified relations. He believes that, by explaining 'the full extent' of the relations of resemblance, contiguity and causation in this way, he has set forth an empirical theory which is adequate to explain all transitions in thought and can serve as a theory of 'a kind of ATTRACTION, which in the mental world will be found to have as extraordinary effects as in the natural' (Hume 1978: 13).

Later Hume refers to the three principles of association as 'natural relations': relations by which the human mind is naturally affected, so that thought slides easily from one to another object when the objects are so related. Of course, there are other relations. The term Hume uses for relations in general is 'philosophical relations'. Thus for Hume any relation is a philosophical relation, but the only natural relations are resemblance, contiguity and causation. This, in a sentence, is Hume's theory of the association of ideas.

The principles of association have an equally important role in Hume's theory of mind in explaining belief. When an impression occurs in the mind it attracts into it an idea that is related to it by one of the three natural relations. For impressions and ideas differ only in vivacity and not in content, and the natural relations hold between ideas in virtue of their contents. But when it is an *impression* that occurs in the mind it not only attracts related ideas into the mind, it also transfers to them a share of its vivacity, it *enlivens* the associated ideas. However, according to Hume, a belief is nothing more than a lively and forceful idea. So if an idea is sufficiently enlivened it becomes a belief. Thus the principles of association, by serving as conduits of vivacity transference, provide Hume with an account of the origin of belief.

However, this account also provides him with a problem with which he struggles in section X of Part III of the *Treatise*. For Hume does *not* wish to allow that all three principles of association can serve equally well to explain belief. Only causation can do so. Thus he has to explain why contiguity and resemblance can never serve as conduits of a sufficient quantity of vivacity to transform an idea into a belief, but only strengthen an already formed belief. His solution to this problem, in brief, is that there is just one (possibly complex) idea to be attracted into the mind by the cause–effect link (since causes are necessary and sufficient conditions of their effects). On the other hand, when resemblance or contiguity function as natural relations, many different ideas will be apt to be pulled into the mind by the associative link, since any thing will resemble several others, and any thing has many neighbours. The vivacity transmitted in these latter cases is *shared out* among the related ideas so that each gets only a portion, insufficient to transform it into a belief. By contrast when the cause–effect relation is serving as the natural relation, since 'the thought is always determined to pass from the impression to the idea, and from that particular impression to that particular idea without any choice or hesitation' (Hume 1978: 110), all the vivacity accrues to a single idea.

We can see why Hume is so determined to deny that contiguity or resemblance can originate belief, if we step outside the confines of his vocabulary and note that belief is a propositional attitude: a belief is a belief *that* something is the case, which may be true or false.

Suppose I have seen Peter and Jane together in the past. Seeing Peter, am I supposed to form the belief *that Jane is in the vicinity?* I might do so if *whenever* (and only whenever) I see Peter I see Jane, but such constant conjunction is precisely, for Hume, what underpins our belief in a causal connection. Observed contiguity without constant conjunction could plainly have no such effect. Nor, of course, could contiguity explain the formation of any other belief about Jane – that she still exists, for example.

The same is true of resemblance. Suppose Peter and Jane are twins. So, in accordance with Hume's views when I think of Peter I am apt to think of Jane, and conversely. What belief should I form when I see Peter? If neither causation nor contiguity is supposed to be operative I cannot form the belief *that Jane is in the vicinity.* But what other belief could I form? *That Jane is somewhere?* Our minds do not work in these ways, and it is to Hume's credit that he recognizes this, despite the inconvenience it causes him.

Abstract ideas

Hume says that our idea of time 'is not derived from a particular impression mix'd up with others and plainly distinguishable from them' (Hume 1978: 36) and from the context it is clear that he would say the same about our idea of space. The idea of existence is similarly said not to be 'derived from any particular impression'

(Hume 1978: 66). Yet Hume employs the Copy Principle critically in the very sections in which these apparent counter-examples are retailed. Thus he denies the existence of ideas of a vacuum and of time without change because there are no impressions from which these ideas can be derived (Hume 1978: 65).

The explanation of the apparent inconsistency is that Hume thinks that the ideas of space, time and existence are genuine ones, because he thinks of them as *abstract*. Whereas, he thinks, we cannot have even an abstract idea of time without change or of empty space.

We need, then, to turn to Hume's theory of abstract ideas in the *Treatise*, summarized in the *Enquiry* by a footnote (Hume 1975: 158).

The notion of an abstract idea is an attempt to make sense of the generality of thought. We can think thoughts about *all men*, and *all triangles*. To Locke, Berkeley and Hume it seemed that to account for such generality we must posit ideas which are *general in their representation*. But how can an idea be general in its representation? How can our idea of man represent equally all men, fat and thin, tall or short? To do so, it seems, it must represent *all* possible human sizes or shapes or *no* particular sizes and shapes at all.

Locke takes the latter option. For him abstract ideas are formed by abstraction, which separates what is in real existence inseparable to produce a sketchy indeterminate idea:

> [children] ... frame an *idea*, which they find many particulars do partake in, and to that they give ... the name *man*. ... *thus they come to have a general name*, and a general *idea*. Wherein they make nothing new, but only leave out of the complex *idea* they had of *Peter* and *James*, *Mary* and *Jane*, that which is peculiar to each, and retain only what is common.

> (*Essay* III, iii.7)

Locke thinks we can achieve the yet more abstract idea of *animal*: 'not by any addition, but ... by leaving out the shape, and some other properties signified by the name *man*, and retaining only a body, with life, sense, and spontaneous motion' (*Essay* III, iii.7).

Berkeley flatly denies that such a process of abstraction is possible:

> the idea of a man that I form to my self, must be of a white, or a black, or a tawny, or a straight, or a crooked, a tall or a low, or a middle sized man. I cannot by any effort of thought conceive the abstract idea above described [i.e. one retaining only what is common to all men].
>
> (Berkeley 1949: 29)

Berkeley believes that such ideas are a logical impossibility. For they must be indeterminate: the abstract idea of a triangle, for example, must be neither equilateral nor not equilateral. But such indeterminate objects cannot exist.

Of course, it is natural to protest that this objection rests on the absurd assumption that an idea of a triangle must itself *be* a triangle. But three points can be made in response. First, arguably, Berkeley did make this assumption. Second, Locke himself writes as if it is correct, for example, in the notorious passage in which, to Berkeley's glee, he refers to 'the general idea of a triangle, [which] must be neither Oblique, nor Rectangle, neither Equilateral, Equicrural, nor Scalenon: but all and none of these at once' (*Essay* IV, vii.9). Third, *Hume* certainly takes it for granted that an idea of a triangle must be triangular: *his* reification of ideas is absolutely self-conscious; and so, as he sees it, if there can be Lockean abstract ideas reality itself can be indeterminate, which is a possibility he rejects out of hand.

Hume begins his discussion of abstract ideas by affirming what he takes to be Berkeley's view: 'all general ideas are nothing but particular ones, annexed to a certain term, which gives them a more extensive signification, and makes them recall upon occasion other individuals which are similar to them' (Hume 1978: 17).

Hume sees the argument for what he takes to be the Lockean position to rest upon a plain dilemma: 'The abstract idea of a man represents men of all sizes and all qualities; which 'tis concluded it cannot do, but either by representing at once all possible sizes and all possible qualities, or by representing no particular one at all' (Hume 1978: 18). But, it seems, the first alternative is impossible since, it seems, it requires an infinite capacity in the mind, so we are left with the second, Lockean, alternative. Yet Hume argues that this involves something 'utterly impossible' – 'to conceive any quantity or quality without forming a precise notion of its degree' (Hume 1978: 18) – and that the first alternative is not impossible after all, since even though the capacity of the mind is not infinite 'we can at once form a notion of all possible degrees of quantity and quality, in such a manner, at least, as, however imperfect, may serve all the purposes of reflexion and conversation' (Hume 1978: 18).

Hume gives three arguments against the Lockean alternative. The first begins with a statement of his Separability Principle and its 'inverse' (what we would call the converse): 'whatever objects are different are distinguishable and that whatever objects are distinguishable are separable by the thought and imagination. And ... these propositions are equally true in the *inverse*, ... whatever objects are separable are also distinguishable, and that whatever objects are distinguishable are also different' (Hume 1978: 18).

Given these principles, Hume argues, the separability of a precise degree of a quality or quantity from that quantity or quality itself is impossible. Taking the relation of the precise length of a line to the line itself as his illustration of the relation between a precise degree of a quantity and the quantity itself, he argues thus:

> [T]he precise length of a line is not different nor distinguishable from the line itself; nor the precise degree of any quantity from the quantity. These ideas, therefore, admit no more of separation than they do of distinction and difference ... the general idea of a line, not withstanding all our abstractions and refinements has in its appearance in the mind a precise degree of quantity and quality; however it may be made to represent others, which have different degrees of length.

> (Hume 1978: 18)

The argument here is that since the length of a line *is* the line itself, by the inverse of the Separability Principle it cannot be distinguishable or separable from the line itself (nothing is separable from itself). So in so far as Lockean abstraction implies such separation, it is impossible. And the same holds generally for the precise degree of any quantity and that quantity; they are inseparable because they are identical.

What is interesting about this argument is its starting point. Hume takes it as evident that the precise length of a line *is* the line itself, that the relation between them is identity. But why? Do we not, in general, distinguish between individuals and their qualities, lines and their lengths, bodies and their shapes, objects and their actions, and is this distinction not all that an opponent of Hume needs?

The answer to this question is that we do, in our ordinary thought and talk, make this distinction, but Hume rejects it. In fact, he explicitly asserts, in the case of each of the three instances just cited (1978: 12, 18, 25) the identity of the items we commonly distinguish, and given his principles he must do so.

To see why this is so we must recall that he accepts not just the Separability Principle but also the Conceivability Principle: 'Whatever is clearly conceived may exist, and whatever is clearly conceived after any manner, may exist after the same manner' (Hume 1978: 233).

These principles are put to use in his crucial argument against the traditional notion of substance as 'something which may exist by itself' that 'this definition agrees to everything that can possibly be conceived; and never will serve to distinguish substance from accident or the soul from its perceptions'. Hume explains:

> For thus I reason. Whatever is clearly conceiv'd may exist, and whatever is clearly conceiv'd after any manner, may exist after the same manner. Again, everything which is different, is distinguishable and everything which is distinguishable is separable by the imagination. My conclusion ... is, that since all our perceptions are different from each other, and from everything else in the universe they are also distinct and separable, and may be considered as separately existent, and may exist separately, and have no need of anything else to support their existence. They are, therefore, substances, as far as this definition explains a substance.
>
> (Hume 1978: 233)

This argument enables us to see why Hume is so confident that the precise length of a line cannot be distinguished from the line, or the degree of any quantity from the quantity. For, on Hume's principles, there are *no* dependent entities. If the length of a line is an object distinct from the line it can exist separately from that line, or any line, and has no need of anything else to support its existence. In general, if qualities are distinct from things they can exist separately from them – like the Cheshire cat's grin. But this Hume thinks is absurd, and this is the basis of his first argument against Lockean abstraction.

Hume's second argument appeals again to one of his fundamental principles, the Copy Principle: 'all our simple ideas in their first appearance are deriv'd from simple impressions, which are correspondent to them, and which they exactly represent' (Hume 1978: 4).

This principle enables him to make a transition from what he takes to be a logical truth about impressions to a corresponding conclusion about ideas.

The logical truth about impresssions, to deny which, Hume claims, includes 'the flattest of all contradictions, *viz* that it is possible for the same thing both to be and not be' (Hume 1978: 19), is 'that no object can appear to the senses; or in other words, that no impression can become present to the mind, without being determined in its degrees both of quantity and quality' (Hume 1978: 19).

To appreciate Hume's confidence here it is important to recall that impressions for Hume are not representations of other (external) things; and they are themselves (the only) possessors of both primary and secondary qualities. Thus, to deny the determinateness of impressions, for Hume, is to acknowledge indeterminacy *in the world*.

But, if the indeterminateness of impressions is a logical absurdity, the same, Hume argues, must be true of that of ideas. For ideas and impressions differ only in degree of vivacity and the conclusion that the indeterminacy of impressions is a logical absurdity was 'not founded upon any particular degree of vivacity' (Hume 1978: 19).

Hume's third argument against Lockean abstract ideas again moves from the impossibility of indeterminacy in the world to the impossibility of indeterminacy in thought, this time via an appeal to the Conceivability Principle.

Since indeterminate objects are impossible we can form no idea of an indeterminate object, otherwise, by the Conceivability Principle they would be possible. But 'to form the idea of an object, and to form an idea simply is the same thing; the reference of the idea to an object being an extraneous denomination which in itself it bears no mark or character' (Hume 1978: 20). Any idea can count as an idea representing an object, in the only sense Hume allows, in virtue of its resemblance to that object (that is, that impression). So, if ideas indeterminate in their own character were possible they would serve as ideas *of* indeterminate objects. But it has already been established that such ideas are impossible. Thus, 'abstract ideas are, therefore, in themselves, individual, however, they may become general in their representation. The image in the mind is only that of a particular object, tho' the application of it in our reasoning be the same, as if it were universal' (Hume 1978: 20).

Thus Hume's rejection of Lockean abstract ideas is not an incidental element in his philosophy, but derives from assumptions and principles which are fundamental to it: the Copy Principle, and the insistence that the *only* difference between impressions and ideas is one of degrees of vivacity; the Separability Principle and the consequent rejection of any dependent entities and the reification of perceptions; the Conceivability Principle and the denial of any distinction between an idea's resembling an object or impression and its representing, or being an idea *of*, that object or impression.

Having rejected Locke's account of general thought, Hume needs to provide his own. He proposes an account that he takes to be an elaboration of Berkeley's. The key point is that general thought is secondary to the use of general terms. For Locke, words become general by being associated with general or abstract ideas; for Hume, ideas become general or abstract by being associated with general terms. Nothing in the mind of a thinker describable without reference to language can make his thought to be general rather than particular.

When we have found a resemblance among several objects, notwithstanding their differences, we apply the same name to all of them. Then, after acquiring a custom of this kind,

> [T]he hearing of that name revives the idea of one of these objects ... and ... that custom, which we have acquired by surveying them. ... The word raises up an individual idea, along with a certain custom, and that custom produces any other individual one, for which we may have occasion.

(1978: 20–21)

Thus, according to Hume it is possible for a particular idea to acquire a general representation by being associated with a term with which is also associated a custom, or disposition, to produce other particular ideas of resembling objects as need be. What makes the idea general, however, is nothing in its intrinsic character, but only the custom with which it is linked via the general term.

Hume thinks that however, in more detail, the custom he describes is to be characterized, it is this alone that can account for general thought. In fact, he admits, the *same* particular idea may occur in the minds of people who are thinking *different* general thoughts. The idea of an equilateral triangle, for example, may be present before the mind of a man who is thinking of equilateral triangles, and one who is thinking of triangles generally, and one who is thinking of all regular figures. The difference between the thoughts will consist in no *actual* difference but in the different dispositions of the three thinkers, their different states of readiness to produce, as need be, ideas of resembling objects. And indeed, even if *no* idea is before the mind, such a state of readiness may be present and will suffice for thought: 'we do not annex distinct and complete ideas to every term we make use of' (Hume 1978: 23) 'it being usual, after the frequent use of terms ... to omit the idea, which we wou'd express by them, and to preserve only the custom by which we recal the idea at pleasure' (Hume 1978: 224).

Hume ends his section on abstract ideas by declaring that he will employ 'the same principles to explain that *distinction of reason* which is so much talked of, and is so little understood, in the schools' (Hume 1978: 24).

Hume begins by giving examples of what is meant by a 'distinction of reason': the distinction between figure and body figured and between motion and body moved. Another example he goes on to discuss is that between the colour and form of a body.

Hume cannot recognize these distinctions as genuine ones: the figure of a body cannot be a distinct object from the body. Otherwise by the Separability Principle it could exist separately and independently of the existence of any body. The same reasoning applies to the other pairs of putatively distinct items. As he puts it himself: 'What then is meant by a distinction of reason, since it implies neither a difference nor separation?' (Hume 1978: 25).

Thus 'distinctions of reason' are an important topic for Hume because as construed 'in the schools' they are distinctions between inseparable entities and thus counter-examples to the Separability Principle.

At this point Hume introduces his own positive account of abstract ideas. Put simply his position is that the ideas connected with the terms 'the figure of body X' and 'body X' are abstract ideas. So there need be *no* actual difference between someone who is thinking of body X and someone who is thinking of the figure of body X; the same particular determinate idea may be before the minds of the two thinkers. But the man who is thinking of the figure of body X will be in a different state of readiness from a man who is thinking of body X itself. The man who is thinking of the figure of body X will be disposed to produce ideas of other bodies, resembling body X in respect of shape; whereas the man who is thinking of body X will not be so disposed, but rather will be disposed to produce ideas of body X itself, differing in respect of shape, but otherwise the same.

Thus, Hume thinks, his account of abstract ideas enables him to explain what 'distinctions of reason' are. They are not distinctions actually present in thought (for any idea which can serve as the abstract idea of a figure will be a particular idea which can equally well serve as the abstract idea of a body). They are, rather, distinctions only made possible through language, and the general thought which language makes possible.

Hume's theory of thought

Hume, like Locke, endorsed an imagistic theory of thought, which, in virtue of the work of Wittgenstein, can now be recognized to be untenable, since any image can be interpreted in more than one way and so no image can determine the identity of the object of thought.

However, in the light of Hume's discussion of abstract ideas we can see that his theory is more complex and insightful than at first appears. Hume can endorse Wittgenstein's famous remark 'If God had looked into my mind he would not have seen there, of whom I was thinking' (Wittgenstein 1968: 217). He can agree that nothing that goes on at a time can constitute a thought with a particular content; that whatever happens in my consciousness when I think a thought places no constraint on the content of my thought; and that no image at at all is necessary for me to think a particular thought.

Nevertheless, the Wittgensteinian critique of the imagistic account of thinking still applies to Hume, even when his theory of abstract ideas is taken into account. For Wittgenstein's main point – that an idea (something whose identity is constituted by what is the case at the time it is before the mind) cannot in itself compel the understanding to take it in one way rather than another – applies equally to any set of items of like character. So Hume's account of what makes my thought to be a thought of a triangle rather than an equilateral triangle or any regular figure when I have before my mind an idea, for example, of an equilateral triangle, namely, that I stand in readiness to recall other particular ideas to mind, cannot explain the determinateness of my thought unless the set of images I associate with the word 'triangle', and which I stand in readiness to recall, is the set of all *possible* triangle images. But to interpret Hume's account in this way is to rob it of all possible empirical import. The theory can pretend to be explanatory only if the associated images are ones which we stand in readiness to *recall* because they are ones we have previously *encountered* – otherwise the notion of 'recall' has lost any empirical meaning.

To illustrate the difficulty consider Wittgenstein's famous example of the incapacity of images to determine their own interpretation. 'I see a picture: it represents an old man walking up a steep path leaning on a stick. How? Might it not have looked just the same if he had been sliding downhill in that position? Perhaps a Martian would describe the picture so' (Wittgenstein 1968: 54).

In other words, we still need an account of what it is to take a picture one way or the other. The intrinsic qualities of the picture do not determine this, but no addition of signs or extra features to the picture will determine a unique interpretation. If we add arrows, for example, to indicate the direction of movement they, too, can be interpreted in different ways. (Maybe the Martians fire their arrows feathered end first.) Whatever we add will just be another sign in as much need of interpretation as the original. And the same will be true if we add a set of resembling images of men walking up hills. Each such image can be interpreted in more than one way, and the whole set taken together can be interpreted in more than one way.

If the image before the mind, then, is one of the mountain scene Wittgenstein describes, it is not determined thereby that I am thinking of 'an old man walking up a hill' – if God were to look into my mind and see that image he would not be able to deduce from its presence that that was the content of my thought. And if somehow a whole array of resembling images were simultaneously *actually* present, the situation would not be any different. Nor then can it be any different if only one image is actually before my mind and the remainder there only 'in power', as Hume puts it.

Thus Hume's theory of thought, despite the Wittgensteinian insights in his account of abstract ideas, fails to explain, in the face of the Wittgensteinian challenge, how determinate thought is possible. This is a failing, however, shared by every theory of thought which has so far been produced. And the challenge must remain unanswered until it is shown how thought (and other intentional states) can at the same time both sustain normative relations to what is external to them and be available to their subjects as occurrent phenomena of consciousness, whose identity is constituted by what is the case at the time of their occurrence – it is this task which Wittgenstein's (1968) 'rule-following considerations' have left to his successors.

Chapter Three

Causation, induction and necessary connection

The grounds of belief and the role of causation

In Part III of Book I of the *Treatise* and sections IV and V of the first *Enquiry* Hume discusses two questions: (1) what 'is the nature of that evidence which assures us of any real existence and matter of fact, beyond the present testimony of our senses, or the records of our memory' (1975: 26), or, in other words, what leads us to form beliefs about unobserved matters of fact, or assures us of 'existences and objects we do not see or feel'? (Hume 1978: 74); and (2) how do we arrive at the knowledge of cause and effect (Hume 1975: 27) and from what origin is our idea of it derived? (Hume 1978: 74).

The questions are connected, Hume thinks, because 'all our reasonings concerning matter of fact seem to be founded on the relation of Cause and Effect' (Hume 1975: 26), the only relation 'that can be trac'd beyond our senses and informs us of existences and objects, which we do not see or feel' (Hume 1978: 74). That is, the answer to question (1) is 'causal inference'.

But is all belief in unobserved matters of fact belief based on causation?

I believe that all bachelors are unmarried, for example, not as a result of causal inference. Again, it is not on the basis of causal inference that I believe that $2 + 2 = 4$, or that, if snow is white and grass is green then snow is white. That is, (i) beliefs based on knowledge of meaning, (ii) beliefs about mathematical facts and (iii) beliefs about logical truths are not products of causal inference. Hume assumes a distinction between beliefs of these three kinds and those to which his thesis applies. This distinction, set out in sections I and II of Part III of the *Treatise* and at the beginning of section IV of the *Enquiry*, is the distinction between propositions based on relations of ideas and propositions, concerning matters of fact, based on relations which 'may be chang'd without any change in the ideas' (Hume 1975: 25, 1978: 69). Beliefs of the kind listed above turn out to be beliefs in propositions based on relations of ideas.

Hume's discussion of this distinction in the *Treatise* is difficult (see Bennett 1971: chapter X). In places he has in mind a distinction between relations between objects that supervene on their non-relational qualities, that is, cannot alter without any alteration in their non-relational qualities, and those that do not. Contiguity and distance are cited as non-supervening relations, which 'may be changed merely by an alteration of their place, without any change on the objects themselves or on their ideas' (Hume 1978: 69), and contrasted with the supervening relations of resemblance and proportions in quantity or number. However, it is not this distinction that really interests him. To understand what does recall that ideas, for Hume, are the materials of thought and double up as meanings. (Plausibly the distinction between supervenient and non-supervenient relations intrudes because ideas are also copies of impressions, impressions are appearances of objects, and how an object appears depends on its non-relational qualities.)

If ideas are meanings, a proposition 'based on relations of ideas' is one whose truth can be seen by reflecting on the meanings of the words used to express it, or what is now called an analytic proposition, and Hume's position can now be formulated as the thesis that all the kinds of proposition listed – (ii) and (iii) as well as (i) – are analytic propositions.

Such propositions need not be obviously true. A complicated arithmetical identity may require many pages of proof. But nonetheless, Hume will say, if it is true at all, it will be true merely in virtue of 'relations of ideas'.

To defend this position Hume borrows from Locke (1961, *Essay* IV ii.1) a distinction between intuition and demonstration (Hume 1975: 25; 1978: 70). An analytic truth like 'All bachelors are unmarried', which can be seen to be true immediately by anyone who understands it, is accessible to intuition. Not so in the case of a complicated mathematical theorem. But, Hume believes, given the proof of the theorem, (a) the starting point and (b) each link will be intuitively evident. Hence the proof shows how the theorem, though not obviously true, is true merely in virtue of relations of ideas. And Hume believes that the truth of all beliefs of the kinds listed above is knowable either by intuition or demonstration.

According to Hume such propositions have several other features:

1. They can be known to be true without appeal to experience. That is, they are knowable a priori, not merely a posteriori.
2. They are necessary truths. It seems fairly obvious that an analytic proposition must state a necessary truth. But the converse is not obvious. Perhaps there are necessary a posteriori truths, which are not analytic, as many recent philosophers, following Kripke (1980) would claim: for example, that water is H_2O, that gold is an element, that I originated from a particular sperm and ovum, or that the table I am now writing on was originally made from a particular piece of wood.
3. They are the only ones that are, strictly speaking, knowable at all. Propositions concerning matters of fact and existence are not knowable but only probable. In this, he again follows Locke. But Hume is aware of the oddity of this contention and acknowledges it: 'one would appear ridiculous, who wou'd say that 'tis only probable the sun will rise tomorrow, or that all men must die' (Hume 1978: 124). So he distinguishes between proofs (arguments from experience that allows no room for uncertainty) and probabilities. But he still insists on the distinction between propositions concerning matters of fact – however

certain – and propositions expressing relations of ideas. Even if someone is as certain that the sun will rise tomorrow as that $1 + 1 = 2$, the difference between the two propositions remains that the latter can be demonstrated and the former not.

Hume sums up the distinction most elegantly in the *Enquiry*:

> All the objects of human reason and enquiry may be divided into two kinds, to wit, Relations of Ideas and Matters of Fact. Of the first kind ... [is] ... every affirmation which is either intuitively or demonstratively certain. ... Propositions of this kind are discoverable by the mere operation of thought, without dependence on what is anywhere existent in the universe. ... Matters of fact. ... are not ascertained in the same manner; nor is our evidence of their truth, however great, of a like nature. ... The contrary of every matter of fact is still possible; because it can never imply a contradiction and is conceived by the mind with the same facility and distinctness, as if ever so conformable to reality.

(Hume 1975: 25)

The idea of cause

In this way, by distinguishing relations of ideas and matters of fact and existence, Hume specifies more exactly the focus of his contention that 'all reasonings concerning matter of fact seem to be founded on the relation of Cause and Effect' (Hume 1975: 26), or as he also expresses it: that no other 'relations can ever be made use of in reasoning, except so far as they either affect or are affected by [causation]' (Hume 1978: 74). And from here he proceeds to his investigation into the origin of our idea of causation.

Hume's approach to this investigation in the *Treatise* is to look for an impression or impressions from which the idea can be derived. He first notes that: 'The idea of causation must be derived from some relation among objects' (Hume 1978: 75). He finds three distinct relations to be involved: contiguity, priority in time and necessary connection. It is the third of these that Hume regards as crucial to causation. He does so because his interest in causation stems from his desire to explain the nature of the inferences we make from the observed to the unobserved. He has already argued that 'we ought not to receive as reasoning any of the observations we ... make concerning ... the relations of time and place; since in none of them the mind can go beyond what is immediately present to the senses, either to discover the real existence or the relations of objects' (Hume 1978: 73).

Since causation does enable the mind to go beyond the senses it cannot do so merely because it entails contiguity and priority in time, which are relations of time and place, but must do so because it entails necessary connection. And, indeed, a necessary connection is at first sight an obvious candidate for grounding such inference: given a perception of an object of a certain type and a perception of a necessary connection with another type of object, it seems that a basis must be provided for an inference to the existence of an unperceived object of the second type.

But Hume now claims, he cannot discover any impression of necessary connection from which the idea may be derived. We perceive the known qualities of the objects we think of as cause and effect, their colours and shapes and sizes, for example, 'but the relation of cause and effect depends not in the least on them' (Hume 1978: 77), and we perceive spatiotemporal relations (contiguity and succession) 'which I have already regarded as imperfect and unsatisfactory' (Hume 1978: 77), and that is all – we do not perceive any necessary connection, or as he puts it in the *Enquiry*, 'any quality which binds the effect to the cause and renders the one an infallible consequence of the other. We only find that the one does, in fact, follow the other' (Hume 1975: 63).

Hume does not at this point in the *Treatise* explain why he is so sure that this is so, though this becomes clearer later in section VI. But consider what it would be like to observe necessary connection. We can observe priority in time and contiguity in time and space when two suitably related objects are presented to us, but Hume writes, 'we call this perception rather than reasoning' (Hume 1978: 73). If inference is to take place only one of the objects can be present to sense. But then the relation (of priority in time or contiguity) will not be present to sense. Necessary connection, if it is to play the role in inference Hume ascribes to it, must be presented to sense both when both the connected objects are presented and also when only one is presented, so that inference to the second is possible. In this respect, it seems, it must be unlike not only contiguity and priority in time but also any other relation. Hume's confidence that no such thing can be observed may now seem somewhat more understandable.

But Hume does not take his failure to find an impression of necessary connection as proof that there can be ideas without prior impressions: 'This would be too strong a proof of levity and inconstancy' (Hume 1978: 77). Instead, 'beat[ing] about all the neighbouring fields' (Hume 1978: 78), he turns from the direct search for the impression of necessary connection to take up two questions: (a) 'For what reason we pronounce it necessary that every thing whose existence has a beginning, shou'd also have a cause' and (b) 'why we conclude that such particular causes must necessarily have such particular effects, and what is the nature of that inference we draw from the one to the other, and of the belief we repose in it?' (Hume 1978: 78), the first in section III and the second in section VI. His discussion is complicated and takes some unexpected turns, but it emerges in the end that the answer to his second question provides the shortest route to the discovery of the sought-for impression.

The Causal Maxim

Hume's question (a) 'Why we pronounce it necessary that every beginning of existence should have a cause?' is the question why we believe what he calls the 'general maxim in philosophy, that whatever begins to exist, must have a cause of existence' (Hume 1978: 78) (hereafter 'the Causal Maxim'). This is the modal proposition that it is a necessary truth that every beginning of existence has a cause. Thus Hume's question (a) is distinct from his question (b) 'Why we [think] that such particular causes must necessarily have such particular effects?' The Causal Maxim could be true without particular causes being necessarily connected to particular effects, or false even if particular causes were necessarily connected to particular effects. Despite this, Hume thinks that the same answer will serve for both questions (Hume 1978: 82). This is because he thinks that the Causal Maxim is false and that there is no necessary connection between particular causes and effects. What explains both beliefs is thus a mere psychological compulsion.

The most important part of Hume's discussion of the Causal Maxim is his attempt to refute it. This appeals to the divide between propositions concerning relations of ideas and the rest. If it is a necessary truth, Hume argues, that every beginning of existence has a cause, it must be either intuitively certain or demonstrable. But it is not intuitively certain, for it is not obviously contradictory to deny it. Nor, however, is it demonstratively certain.

Hume attempts to prove this point by an argument from imagination:

[A]s all distinct ideas are separable from each other, and as the ideas of cause and effect are evidently distinct, 'twill be easy for us to conceive any object to be non-existent this moment, and existent the next, without conjoining to it the distinct idea of a cause or productive principle. The separation, therefore, of the idea of a cause from that of a beginning of existence, is plainly possible for the imagination; and consequently the actual separation of these objects is so far possible, that it implies no contradiction nor absurdity; and is therefore incapable of being refuted by any reasoning from mere ideas; without which 'tis impossible to demonstrate the necessity of a cause.

(Hume 1978: 79–80)

Here Hume appeals to the combination of the Separability Principle and the Conceivability Principle. The argument is that a cause is a distinct object from its effect. So it is distinguishable and separable by the imagination. Consequently the actual separation of the objects is possible and that object which is, in fact, the effect (the 'beginning of existence') may exist without need of any cause.

The argument is fallacious. Given the Separability and Conceivability Principles any object X, whose coming into existence is the effect of a particular cause C, might have come into existence in the absence of C. But it does not follow that X might have come into existence without any cause. For it is compatible with the argument that in order for X to exist some cause must bring it into existence even if there is no particular cause which must bring X into existence if X is brought into existence.

Thus Hume's first argument against the Causal Maxim actually moves his case forward not at all. But if the Causal Maxim is a truth then the necessity of a cause to any beginning of existence must be demonstrable. In the second part of section III Hume goes on to examine four purported demonstrations, from Hobbes, Samuel Clarke, Locke and an unnamed other and argues convincingly that in each case it fails.

He then sums up: he takes himself (mistakenly) to have shown that there can be no intuitive or demonstrative knowledge that every event has a cause, and hence that belief in the Causal Maxim must arise, not from reason, but from experience – which leads us astray (because experience cannot establish that it is a necessary truth that every event has a cause; Hume never questions that it is in fact true). The next question Hume asks is this: how can experience give rise to such a principle? And this question he now proposes to sink into the second question identified earlier 'in the neighbouring fields': why do we conclude that such particular causes must necessarily have such particular effects and why do we form an inference from one to the other? This is our next topic.

Inference from the observed to the unobserved

Hume moves to the crucial part of his discussion in section VI, and here it will be useful to have before us a brief overview of the general shape of his ensuing argument.

First, he argues that observation of any single event, considered it in itself, cannot provide us with a basis for belief that another specific type of event will follow. Hence, he argues, past experience is the necessary foundation for causal inference. But we can have no reason to expect the future to resemble the past since any argument for this general principle will necessarily be circular. Consequently, just as it is not reason which convinces us of the truth of the Causal Maxim, so it is not reason which convinces us that there are necessary connections between particular causes and particular effects in virtue of which we are entitled to infer the effect on observing the cause: 'When the mind, therefore, passes from the idea or impression of one object to the idea or belief of another, it is not determined by reason, but by certain principles, which associate together the ideas of these objects, and unite them in the imagination' (Hume 1978: 92), or, as he puts it in the *Enquiry*, 'it is not reasoning which engages us to suppose the past resembles the future, and to expect similar effects from causes which are, to appearance, similar' (1975: 39).

Finally, Hume returns in section XIV to the question that initiated his enquiry: whence arises the idea of necessary connection? He answers that since there is no necessary connection between the objects that are causes and effects, no necessity 'in the world' as we might say, the ideas of the cause and effect must be simply bound together in our minds as a result of our past experience. Hence necessity is something that exists only in our minds, not in the objects themselves. Thus it is only in the mind that the impression of necessary connection is to be found, where it occurs as an accompaniment to our causal inferences. And it is from this impression that we derive the idea of necessity at the heart of our idea of causation.

With this brief overview let us now return to the starting point of Hume's argument: the contention, in the first paragraph of section VI, that 'there is no object, which implies the existence of any other if we consider these objects in themselves and never look beyond the ideas which we form of them' (Hume 1978: 86–7). It is because he is convinced of this that he is confident that we receive no impression of necessary connection from the objects: the objects are not necessarily connected so there is no suitable relation between them for there to be an impression of.

This contention is thus a crucial one for Hume and in making it he is putting himself against a massive philosophical tradition to be found on both sides of the so-called 'divide' between Empiricists and Rationalists.

We have already noted, in the first chapter, Malebranche's definition of a 'true cause': one such that the mind perceives a necessary connection between it and its effect.

In Spinoza (1949) we find (Axiom 3, Book I of the *Ethics*) 'From a given determinate cause an effect necessarily follows; and, on the other hand, if no determinate cause be given it is impossible that an effect can follow' (Spinoza 1949: 42).

In Hobbes' *Elements of Philosophy Concerning Body*, chapter IX:

> A CAUSE simply, or an entire cause is the aggregate of all the accidents both of the agents how many so ever they be, and of the patients, put together, which when they are supposed to be present, it cannot be understood but that the effect is produced at the same instant; and if any one of them be absent it cannot be understood but that the effect is not produced.

> (Hobbes 1994: 121)

The idea, expressed most explicitly in this last passage, that a cause–effect link must be something which can be understood, rather than something which must just be accepted as a brute fact, is what Hume is most opposed to. One way in which this idea can surface in a philosopher's writings, as we have seen, is in the contention that causes and effects are necessarily connected. But another expression of the same idea is that causes and effects must have some likeness or common feature which allows us to see how they can be linked.

Thus Descartes (the *Third Meditation*): 'it is manifest by the natural light of nature that there must be at least as much reality in the efficient and total cause as in the effect. For where, I ask, would the effect get its reality from, if not the cause? And how could the cause give it to the effect unless it possessed it?' (Descartes 1984: 28).

This principle underlies Descartes' first argument for the existence of God, and Locke (1961) argues similarly 'whatsoever is first of all things must necessarily contain ... all the perfections that can ever after exist; nor can it ever give to another any perfection that it hath not ...: it necessarily follows that the first eternal being cannot be matter' (*Essay*, IV, x.8).

Hume's other chief empiricist predecessor, Berkeley, similarly argues that causes and effects must have something in common. It is an 'old known axiom', he thinks, that 'nothing can give to another that which it hath not itself' (Berkeley 1949: 236n).

And so he is easily able to conclude 'That a being endowed with knowledge and will, should produce or exhibit ideas is easily understood. But that a being which is utterly destitute of these faculties should be able to produce ideas, or in any sort to affect an intelligence, this I can never understand' (Berkeley 1949: 242).

Against this, Hume's position is that 'any thing may produce any thing' (Hume 1978: 173). Causation is never more than a brute fact. It is only through experience that we can learn what causes operate in the world: 'There are no objects which by the mere survey, without consulting experience, we can determine to be the causes of any other, and no objects which we can certainly determine in the same manner not to be the causes' (Hume 1978: 173).

Thus, as Hume puts it in the Abstract:

> Were a man such as Adam created in the full vigour of under-standing, without experience, he would never be able to infer motion in the second ball from the motion and impulse of the first. It is not anything that reason sees in the cause, which makes us infer the effect.

(Hume 1978: 650)

And in the *Enquiry*: 'Nor can our reason, unassisted by experience, ever draw any inference concerning real existence and matter of fact' (Hume 1975: 27).

Hume takes himself to have established all this in the first paragraph of section VI. However, his argument for it is simply another appeal (as in section III) to the conjunction of the Separability and Conceivability Principles. Causes and effects are distinct events and thus, by the conjunction of these principles, either might occur in the absence of the other. In the *Enquiry* the Separability Principle is not explicitly formulated, but it is implicit at the corresponding part of the argument, as Hume's emphasis on the distinctness of the objects that are causes and effects shows:

> The mind can never possibly find the effect in the supposed cause, by the most accurate scrutiny and examination. For the effect is totally different from the cause, and consequently can never be discovered in it. Motion in the second billiard ball is a quite distinct event from motion in the first; nor is there anything in the one to suggest the smallest hint of the other.
>
> (Hume 1975: 29)

> In a word, then, every effect is a distinct event from the cause. It could not, therefore, be discovered in the cause, and the first conception or invention of it, a priori, must be entirely arbitrary.
>
> (Hume 1975: 30)

Of course, there will be many different descriptions of the cause and many different descriptions of the effect, and propositions asserting the occurrence of the cause under some descriptions will entail propositions asserting the existence of the effect under some descriptions. But Hume is not making a claim about propositional entailments. His claim is that the very object which is the cause might have existed in a world in which the very object which is the effect did not exist, and conversely. Thus his contention is that the objects themselves that are causes and effects are not necessarily connected (see also Bennett 2001: 253–5).

Hume now moves on to the next stage of his argument: 'In vain, therefore, should we pretend to determine any single event, or infer any cause or effect, without the assistance of observation and experience' (Hume 1975: 30).

> 'Tis ... by experience only that we can infer the existence of one object from that of another. ... We remember to have had frequent instances of the existence of one species of objects; and also remember, that the individuals of another species of objects have always attended them, ... in a regular order of contiguity and succession with regard to them. Thus we remember to have seen that species of object we call flame and to have felt that species of sensation we call heat. We likewise call to mind their constant

conjunction in all past instances. Without any farther ceremony, we call the one cause and the other effect, and infer the one ... from ... the other.

(Hume 1978: 87; see also 1975: 74)

So we infer B's from A's and pronounce A's the cause of B's when we have experienced A's constantly conjoined with B's.

However, as Hume immediately points out, it is not clear that this is progress. For if an impression of necessary connection is not discernible between a single pair of objects related as cause and effect then equally it cannot be discernible between any exactly resembling pairs – otherwise they would not be exactly resembling: 'There is nothing in a number of instances, different from every single instance, which is supposed to be exactly similar' (Hume 1975: 75; see also 1978: 88).

But Hume hints that the discovery of constant conjunction will nevertheless lead him to his goal:

[H]aving found, that after the discovery of the constant conjunction of any objects we always draw an inference from one object to another, we shall now examine the nature of that inference, and of the transition from the impression to the idea. Perhaps 'twill appear in the end that the necessary connexion depends on the inference, instead of the inference's depending on the necessary connexion.

(Hume 1978: 88)

The next few paragraphs, in which Hume 'examines the nature of that inference', contain his most famous argument. This was traditionally interpreted during most of the twentieth century as Hume's 'sceptical condemnation of induction', that is, as an argument that when we infer the existence of an unobserved effect from an observed cause (or vice versa), on the basis of experience of the constant conjunction of such events, our conclusion is unwarranted, our belief unreasonable, our mode of inference unjustifiable.

Thus Stroud writes:

[Hume] rejects 'reason' or 'the understanding' as the source of such [causal] inferences on the grounds that none of them are ever reasonable. ... Past and present experiences give us ... no reason at all to believe anything about the unobserved. ... As far as the competition for degrees of reasonableness is concerned, all possible beliefs about the unobserved are tied for last place.

(Stroud 1977: 52–4)

Some other interpreters, reacting against this sceptical interpretation, read Hume differently. All he is arguing, they claim, is that if 'reason' is interpreted in a narrow, rationalistic way, which conforms to the deductivist assumption that only valid deductive arguments are any good, then reason has nothing to do with our formation of beliefs about unobserved effects or causes on the basis of observed causes and effects (see Broughton 1983; Beauchamp and Rosenberg 1981). But if so, they suggest that he thought, so much the worse for the deductivist conception of reason.

If we turn to Hume's text this issue of interpretation can be resolved.

Hume begins his examination of causal inference in the *Treatise* by asking 'Whether experience produces the idea by means of the understanding or of the imagination; whether we are determined by reason to make the transition, or by a certain association and relation of perceptions' (Hume 1978: 88–9).

In the *Enquiry* he declares that his aim is to establish that 'Even after we have experience of the operations of cause and effect, our conclusions from that experience are not founded on reasoning, or any process of the understanding' (Hume 1975: 32).

In the *Treatise* he finally answers his question thus: 'When the mind ... passes from the idea or impression of one object to the idea or belief of another it is not determined by reason, but by certain principles which associate together the ideas of these objects and unite them in the imagination' (Hume 1978: 92).

And in the *Enquiry* his statement of his conclusion is 'All inferences from experience, therefore, are effects of custom, not of reasoning' (Hume 1975: 43).

That this is so, Hume thinks, can be established as follows. If reason did determine us 'it wou'd proceed upon' the principle (usually referred to as the Uniformity Principle) that 'instances of which we have had no experience, must resemble those of which we have had experience, and that the course of nature continues always uniformly the same' (Hume 1978: 89).

But there can be no demonstrative arguments for the Uniformity Principle 'since it implies no contradiction that the course of nature may change' (Hume 1975: 35), whilst probable arguments for it must run into a circle since 'probability is founded on the presumption of a resemblance betwixt those objects, of which we have had experience, and those of which we have had none; and therefore 'tis impossible this presumption can arise from probability. The same principle cannot be both the cause and effect of another' (Hume 1978: 90).

Or, in the words of the *Enquiry*:

> All our experimental conclusions proceed upon the supposition that the future will be conformable to the past. To endeavour, therefore, the proof of this last supposition by any probable arguments, or arguments regarding existence, must evidently be going in a circle, and taking for granted, which is the very point in question.
>
> (Hume 1975: 35–6)

Since the Uniformity Principle cannot be established without circularity, and if reason determines us, that is, if our inferences from experiences are the effects of reasoning, it must proceed upon it, it follows that reason does not determine us, that is, that our causal inferences are not the effects of reasoning.

Thus the argument, largely in Hume's own words. But what does it mean?

A way of interpreting it, which stays close to the text, but neither reads the traditional radical scepticism about induction into Hume, nor reads him only as attacking a narrowly rationalistic sense of reason, is to take the causal language in it literally. (This literalist interpretation is suggested by Connon [1979], Broughton [1983], and Garrett [1997], and is also implicit in Loeb [1991; 1995a, b].)

As Hume explains, we engage in the practice of inductive inference, of making inferences from observed events, via beliefs about causes and effects based on past experience, to beliefs about unobserved events. Do we do so because we recognize an argument to the effect that such a practice is in some sense a justified one? That is, is our engaging in the practice of inductive inference itself the causal upshot of our recognizing an argument that it is justified? On the proposed literalist interpretation this is the meaning of Hume's *Treatise* question 'Does reason determine us?' and his assertion in the *Enquiry* that inferences from experience are not the 'effects of reasoning' (Hume 1975: 43) means exactly what it says.

Hume's argument is now that we can be determined by reason, in this sense, only if we infer that it is justified to engage in inductive inference from the Uniformity Principle, the principle that the future will resemble the past. This is the meaning of the claim that 'if reason determin'd us it would proceed upon that principle' (Hume 1978: 89). That is, if our practice of inductive inference is the effect of our accepting an argument that it is justified, a premise of that argument must be the Uniformity Principle.

However, Hume thinks, our acceptance of such an argument could be the cause of our engaging in the practice of inductive inference only if we had a basis for the Uniformity Principle in the form of an argument of which it was the conclusion. We could not be caused to engage in the practice of inductive inference by our acceptance of an argument from the Uniformity Principle, unless we also had an argument for the Uniformity Principle (for we could not believe the Uniformity Principle, antecedently to acquiring a disposition to engage in inductive inference, except on the basis of argument).

But we could not have a demonstrative argument for the Uniformity Principle, since there is no contradiction in denying that the future will be like the past (Hume 1975: 75; 1978: 89).

So any sound argument for the Uniformity Principle must be a probable argument (and since Hume takes it for granted that our practice of inductive inference is justified, as we shall see immediately below, it is only sound arguments he has in view). Now we can indeed accept the Uniformity Principle on the basis of such an argument. We can argue:

In the past, the future has resembled the past.

Therefore, in the future, the future will resemble the past.

But we will be prepared to reason in this way only if we are already disposed to engage in the practice of inductive inference.

However, in that case our acceptance of the Uniformity Principle as the result of so reasoning cannot be the cause of our being disposed to engage in the practice of inductive inference. For 'the same principle cannot be both the cause and effect of another' (Hume 1978: 90).

It cannot, therefore, be reason, that is, our acceptance either of a demonstrative or a probable argument, that determines us to engage in the practice of inductive inference. Rather it must be merely 'custom' (Hume 1975: 43) or 'a certain association and relation of perceptions' (Hume 1978: 89).

On this literalist interpretation 'reason' does not have to be understood in a narrow rationalistic sense, on which it is restricted to what Hume calls 'demonstrative reasoning', to make sense of the argument. Hence the fact that Hume argues that our acceptance of the Uniformity Principle cannot be based on probable reasoning (if 'reason' is to determine the mind's activity) is easily understood. For interpreters who take Hume's argument to be using 'reason' in the narrow way, however, the existence of this stage in the argument is an embarrassment.

Perhaps the most compelling piece of textual evidence for this literalist interpretation of Hume's discussion is in the first *Enquiry* (section IV, Part II), in Hume's summary of the purpose of his argument:

> It is certain that the most ignorant peasants – nay infants, nay even brute beasts – improve by experience, and learn the qualities of natural objects, by observing the effects which result from them. When a child has felt the sensation of pain from touching the flame of a candle, he ... will expect a similar effect from a cause which is similar. ... If you assert, therefore, that the understanding of the child is led into this conclusion by any process of argument ..., I may justly require you to produce that argument. ... If you hesitate ..., or, if, after reflection, you produce any intricate or profound argument, you, in a manner, give up the question, and confess that

it is not reasoning which engages us to suppose the past resembling the future, and to expect similar effects from causes which are, to appearances, similar. This is the proposition which I intended to enforce in the present section.

(Hume 1975: 39)

There are also many passages in the *Treatise* that support the literalist interpretation. In particular, it has no difficulty in making sense of the many passages, both in section VI and subsequently, in which Hume writes as if causal inference is indeed a process of reasoning, and its products products of reason.

It also, unlike the traditional sceptical interpretation, is not in conflict with the many passages in which Hume shows that he regards causal inference as justified. For example, in the very paragraph in which Hume draws the conclusion that ' 'tis impossible this presumption [the Uniformity Principle] can arise from probability' (Hume 1978: 90) he describes cause and effect as the 'only connexion or relation of objects ... on which we can found a *just* inference from one object to another' (Hume 1978: 89, my italics). Again in section VII of Part III, on the same page on which he writes in the text 'when we pass from the impression of one [object] to the idea or belief of another, we are not determined by reason', we find in a footnote, 'We infer a cause immediately from its effect; and this inference is not only a true species of reasoning, but the strongest of all others' (Hume 1978: 97).

On the basis of these passages, and many others, the reading of Hume as a sceptic who denies any distinction between good and bad reasoning and, in particular, denies that causal inference is any better than any other mechanism of belief formations, must be rejected. However, Hume is a sceptic, but the basis for his scepticism only emerges in Part IV, in sections III and IV, and it is quite different from that proposed by the traditional interpretation.

In section III, 'Of the ancient philosophy', Hume turns to an examination of the psychological mechanism that led the ancient philosophers to their belief in the 'unreasonable and capricious' fictions (Hume 1978: 219) of substances, forms, accidents and occult qualities, and caused them to produce a system of philosophy which is 'entirely incomprehensible' (Hume 1978: 224). In section IV, 'Of the modern philosophy', he begins by responding to an objection which he thinks these criticisms of the ancient philosophers might prompt: 'the imagination, according to my own confession, being the ultimate judge of all systems of philosophy, I am unjust in blaming the ancient philosophers for making use of that faculty, and allowing themselves to be entirely guided by it in their reasonings' (Hume 1978: 225).

Hume responds by explicitly making a distinction which he has in fact already been employing consistently and is stated in a footnote in Part III (Hume 1978: 117) between the two sets of imaginative principles:

> [T]he principles which are permanent, irresistable, and universal; such as the customary transition from causes and effects, and from effects to causes; and the principles, which are changeable, weak and irregular; such as those I have just now taken notice of. The former are the foundation of all our thoughts and actions, so that upon their removal human nature must immediately perish and go to ruin. The latter are neither unavoidable to mankind, nor necessary, or so much as useful in the conduct of life; but on the contrary are observ'd only to take place in weak minds, and being opposite to the other principles of custom and reasoning, may easily be subverted by a due contrast and opposition. For this reason the former are received by philosophy and the latter rejected.
>
> (Hume 1978: 225)

Here Hume provides a basis for his preference for causal inference over the mechanisms of belief formation he criticizes the ancient philosophers for employing, and refuses to dignify with the title 'reasoning'. The former belongs to imagination only in the wide, normatively neutral sense distinguished in the Part III footnote and is an indispensable component of our psychology and irresistible in its action; the latter, which belongs to imagination in the narrow, disreputable, sense distinguished in the footnote, is neither. So the ancient philosophers can rightly be criticized for their incomprehensible systems. 'A little reflection' (Hume 1978: 224) was all that was needed to suppress the inclinations that led them to their fantasies.

Thus, Hume can say, though both causal inference and the mechanism of the imagination which leads the ancient philosophers to their fictions are both components of our human nature, they can be distinguished:

> One who concludes somebody to be near him, when he hears an articulate voice in the dark, reasons justly and naturally; tho' that conclusion be derived from nothing but custom ... on account of [the] usual conjunction with the present impression. But one, who is tormented he knows not why, with the apprehension of spectres in the dark, may, perhaps, be said to reason, and to reason naturally, too: But then it must be in the same sense, that a malady is said to be natural; as arising from natural causes, tho' it be contrary to health, the most agreeable and natural situation of man. ... The opinions of the ancient philosophers ... are like the spectres in the dark, and are derived from principles which are ... neither universal nor unavoidable in human nature.
>
> (Hume 1978: 225–6)

But as section III proceeds it emerges that the non-causal mechanisms of the narrow imagination which produce the ancient philosophers' belief in the fictions of substance and accident are identical with those that produce our belief in an external world. But belief in an external world, as Hume has explained in section II, 'Of scepticism with regard to the senses', far from being something which can be suppressed by a little reflection, is inescapable: 'Nature has not left that to ... choice' (Hume 1978: 187). The mechanisms of the narrow imagination in question are therefore permanent, irresistible and unavoidable, after all, and the foundation of Hume's division between the principles 'received by philosophers' and those which are not is undermined. Moreover, it turns out in section IV that causal inference not only does not provide support for our belief in an external world, but further, directly opposes that belief: 'there is a direct and total opposition betwixt our reason and our sense; or more properly speaking, betwixt those conclusions we form from cause and effect, and those that persuade us of the continu'd and independent existence of body' (Hume 1978: 231).

Thus, Hume concludes, two sets of psychological mechanisms are directly opposed: those, on the one hand, that he had previously been happy to describe as processes of reasoning, including causal inference, and those, on the other hand, that he had previously ascribed to disreputable narrow imagination, and had regarded as operative only on weak minds. Both are irresistible in their influence and so no distinction can be drawn between them. So, indeed, no belief can be regarded as more justified than any other.

This is the basis of Hume's scepticism in Part IV. And in its final section, in which he tries to find a way forward past the 'manifold contradictions and imperfections in human reason' (Hume 1978: 268) he has uncovered, it is the conflict exposed in section IV of Part IV (to which a footnote refers us), rather than the argument of section VI of Part III, as the traditional sceptical interpretation would lead us to expect, which is the starting point of his descent into pessimism.

Hume is no sceptic about induction, then, either in the *Treatise* or the *Enquiry*. But now need to consider the positive phase of his account of the manner in which we extend our beliefs to unobserved matters of fact.

The nature and causes of belief

So far Hume's conclusion is that it is not reasoning but custom that engages us to make causal inferences.

It is just a fact about human beings that they are so constituted that experience of a constant conjunction of A's and B's creates in them a disposition to form an idea of an A when presented with an idea of a B. This disposition is not a rational creation of the mind, and, in particular, Hume stresses, it is not a result of the mind's noting or reflecting on the fact that all A's have been conjoined with B's. The bare fact of the occurrence of that pattern in experience, independently of its being known or reflected on, suffices to create the disposition:

> [T]he past experience on which all our judgements concerning cause and effect depend, may operate on the mind in such an insensible manner as never to be taken notice of and may even, in some sense, be unknown to us. ... The custom operates before we have time for reflexion. ... we must necessarily acknowledge that experience may produce a belief and a judgement of causes and effects by a secret operation, and without once being thought of. This removes all pretext ... for asserting that the mind is convinc'd by reasoning of that principle, that instances of which we have no experience, must necessarily resemble those of which we have.
>
> (Hume 1978: 103–4)

Hume reinforces this point in the final section of Part III, of the *Treatise*, 'Of the reason of animals', and in the identically titled section IX of the *Enquiry*. Like men, animals learn many things from experience, in adopting means to ends in seeking self-preservation, obtaining pleasure and avoiding pain. The ignorance and inexperience of the young are here plainly distinguishable from the cunning and sagacity of the old. And, Hume says, 'any theory by which we explain the operations of the understanding, or the origin and connexion of the passions in man, will acquire additional authority, if we find, that the same theory is requisite to explain the same phenomena in all other animals' (Hume 1975: 104). But animals, like men, infer facts beyond what immediately strikes the senses:

> It is impossible that this inference of the animal can be founded in any process of argument or reasoning, by which he concludes, that like events must follow like events. ... Animals, therefore, are not guided in these inferences by reasoning: Neither are children: Neither are the generality of mankind. ... Neither are the philosophers themselves who are ... in the main, the same with the vulgar. Were this doubtful with regard to men, it seems to admit of no question with regard to brute creation; and ... we have a strong presumption, from all the rules of analogy, that it ought to be universally admitted without ... reserve. It is custom alone, which engages

animals from every object ... to infer its usual attendant. ... No
other explication can be given of this operation in all the higher, as
well as lower classes of sensitive beings, which fall under our notice
and observation.

(Hume 1975: 106–7)

So far, however, Hume has only explained how an idea of a
B will occur to a man who has been exposed to a constant conjunction of A's and B's when an idea of an A is present to his mind.
But when a man gets on impression of an A he will not just form
the idea of a B – a belief that a B will occur will come to be present
in his mind. Hence, Hume needs to explain how that happens, and
to do that he has to explain how a belief differs from a mere idea.
This is the task of section VII of Part III of Book I of the *Treatise*
and Part II of section V of the *Enquiry*.

In fact, there are three notions to be considered. First, there is
the mere thinking about something, or conception. Second, there
is the entertaining in thought of a propositional content – that
something is the case. And finally there is belief. Hume conflates
the first two because, in general, he cannot distinguish complex
ideas and propositions, and, in the particular case of existential
propositions, he cannot distinguish simple ideas from propositions since he denies any distinct idea of existence and therefore
insists that we can form a proposition containing only one idea
(Hume 1978: 97). Thus his enquiry is directed at the distinction
between, on the one hand, thinking about something or entertaining a propositional content (not distinguished) and, on the
other hand, believing that something is the case. It is this question
he formulates as 'Wherein consists the difference betwixt a fiction
and belief?' (Hume 1975: 47).

The difference cannot be, he argues, that believing something
as opposed to merely entertaining an idea or proposition involves
the presence of an extra idea – perhaps the idea of existence or
reality. The thought that P and the belief that P do not differ in
their content. When I move from doubting whether P to believing
that P what I later believe is the very same thing that I previously
doubted. Moreover, there is no idea whose addition to others

could make the difference between merely entertaining a thought and believing it. Even if there is a genuine distinct idea of existence (which Hume denies), it could not accomplish this. For one can entertain the thought that God exists as easily as believing that God exists. Furthermore, Hume argues, as the mind has authority over all its ideas 'it could voluntarily annex this particular idea to any fiction, and consequently be able to believe whatever it pleases' (Hume 1978: 653).

Thus, Hume concludes, the difference between merely entertaining a thought and believing it cannot be a difference in content; it can only be a difference in the manner of conception and feeling to the mind (Hume 1975: 49). But, Hume now goes on, the only variation an idea can survive without being changed into another idea is a variation in degree of force or vivacity, hence 'belief is nothing but a more vivid, lively, forcible, firm, steady conception of an object than what the imagination alone is ever able to attain' (1975: 49). And since the extra vivacity derives from a present impression in the case of beliefs resulting from causal inference, in the *Treatise* Hume brings the reference to its origin into his definition of belief: 'An opinion, therefore, or belief, may be most accurately defin'd, A LIVELY IDEA RELATED TO OR ASSOCI-ATED WITH A PRESENT IMPRESSION' (Hume 1978: 96).

It is hard not to feel dissatisfied with this account of belief, and Hume himself indicates his dissatisfaction with it in the Appendix to the *Treatise*, and in the *Enquiry* insists that it is 'impossible perfectly to explain this feeling or manner of conception' (Hume 1975: 49). In the body of the *Treatise*, however, Hume claims that the definition 'is entirely conformable to everyone's feeling and experience' (Hume 1978: 97). But his attempt to illustrate it only brings out the inadequacy of the language in which he attempts to express the distinction:

> If one person sits down to read a book as a romance and another as a true history ... [t]he latter has a more lively conception of all the incidents. He enters deeper into the concerns of the persons; represents to himself their actions and characters and friendships and enmities: he even goes so far as to form a notion of their features, and air and person. While the former, who gives no credit

to the testimony of the author, has a more faint and languid conception of all these particulars, and except on account of the style and ingenuity of the composition can receive little entertainment from it.

(Hume 1978: 17–18)

But, of course, a person reading a fiction need not have such a 'faint and languid conception' of the incidents as Hume here supposes; of course, he may form a notion of the 'features and air and person' of the characters and 'represent to himself their actions and characters, friendships and enmities'. If we understand the notions of vividness and liveliness in any familiar sense, then, Hume's account is woefully inadequate.

There are additional problems. One is that Hume is using the same notion of vivacity to distinguish beliefs from ideas as he previously used to distinguish impressions from ideas. So the degree of vivacity of beliefs must fall somewhat in between that of impressions and ideas. But where, exactly? What degree of vivacity marks the boundary between an impression and a belief, and what degree marks the boundary between a belief and an idea? Hume simply does not say, and, of course, nothing in his system can provide any basis for decision, since the notion of vivacity remains wholly metaphorical.

Nevertheless, despite these difficulties with his definition of belief as a vivid idea, it is an important part, for Hume, of his explanation of what is involved in causal inference. For it enables him to explain the transition from the observation of a cause to the belief in the effect as a case of a more general phenomenon: vivacity communication via the association of ideas. He offers 'a general maxim in the science of human nature that when any impression becomes present to us, it not only transports the mind to such ideas as are related to it, but likewise communicates to them a share of its force and vivacity' (Hume 1978: 98).

Notice that this principle can only explain the origin of belief if beliefs are distinguished from mere ideas by the possession, in a higher degree, of a quality that is also possessed, in a still higher degree, by impressions. Thus, despite the absurdity of trying to describe the differences among ideas, beliefs, memories and impressions, by locating them within different regions of a one-dimensional scale measuring 'degrees of vivacity', this is precisely what Hume needs to do if he is to achieve the explanatory object-ives he sets himself in the *Treatise*.

Section VIII of Part III argues for and illustrates the general principle of vivacity transference. Hume argues that not only the cause–effect link (revealed, by now, to be dependent on observed constant conjunction), but also the two other principles of associ-ation, resemblance and contiguity, can produce an enlivening of ideas. But he insists that these other two principles cannot suffi-ciently enliven an associated idea to transform it into a belief. For otherwise it would not be the case that: '['t]is only causation, which produces such a connexion, as to give us assurance, from the existence or action of one object, that 'twas followed or pre-ceded by any other existence or action' (Hume 1978: 73–4).

The explanation of this difference, Hume suggests, is, in essence, that causes are necessary and sufficient conditions of their effects. Thus, 'There is no manner of necessity for the mind to feign any resembling, and contiguous object; and if it feigns such, there is so little necessity for it always to confine itself to the same, without any difference or variation' (Hume 1978: 109).

But the 'relation of cause and effect':

[H]as all the opposite advantages. The objects it presents are fixt and unalterable ... each impression draws along with it a precise idea, which takes its place in the imagination, as something solid and real, certain and invariable. The thought is always determin'd to pass from the impression to the idea, and from that particular impression to that particular idea, without any choice or hesitation.

(Hume 1978: 110)

But, Hume insists, though causal inference is a special case, trans-itions made via resemblance and contiguity can still add to the liveliness of ideas, and where such an additional effect is not present belief is correspondingly less firm and hesitant.

He finds here an explanation of the hold on philosophers of the belief that causes and effects must be resembling and necessarily connected. Where causes and effects are resembling, as in the communication of motion by impulse, our belief in the effect, given the cause, is greatly strengthened and in consequence 'some philosophers have imagin'd ... that a reasonable man might immediately infer the motion of one object from the impulse of another, without having recourse to any past observation' (Hume 1978: 111). But really this is not so; it is just another illustration of the vivacity-transferring power of resemblance. On the other hand, where cause and effect are not resembling, the opposite effect occurs, '[a]s resemblance, where conjoin'd with causation, fortifies our reasonings; so the want of it in any very great degree is able almost entirely to destroy them' (Hume 1978: 113), and some may find it impossible to believe that there is a causal link at all.

This, then, in sum, is Hume's account of how our beliefs in matters of fact are to be explained. They are not, at bottom, a product of reasoning, but of the imagination. They are derived from nothing but custom, and belief 'is more properly an act of the sensitive than of the cogitative part of our natures' (Hume 1978: 183).

The idea of necessary connection

In explaining why he planned to concentrate on the inference from the observed to the unobserved Hume hinted that: 'Perhaps 'twill appear in the end, that the necessary connexion depends on the inference, instead of the inference depending on the necessary connexion' (Hume 1978: 88). Of course, this is just how it does turn out.

In each instance of a causal connection we simply observe one thing following another, and we get no impression of necessary connection. 'All events seem entirely loose and separate. One event follows another; but we never can observe any tie between them. They seem conjoined but never connected' (Hume 1975: 74). Only after repeated observations of instances of the cause–effect link do we get the idea of necessary connection. But:

> ['T]is evident ... that the repetition of like objects in like relations of succession and contiguity discovers nothing new in any one of them. ... Secondly, 'Tis certain that this repetition of similar

objects ... produces nothing new either in these objects, or in any external body. For ... the several instances we have of the conjunction of resembling causes and effects are in themselves entirely independent. ... They are entirely divided by time and place: and the one might have existed ... tho' the other never had been in being.

(Hume 1978: 81, see also 1975: 75)

How then can the observation of repeated instances of a cause–effect link explain the origin of the idea of necessary connection? Hume's answer is that though the several resembling instances can 'never produce any new quality in the object, yet the observation of this resemblance, produces a new impression in the mind, which is its real model' (Hume 1978: 165).

This new impression is an impression of reflection, an accompaniment of the transition in the mind that takes place, after an observed constant conjunction, from the idea or impression of the cause to the idea of, or belief in, the effect.

In Hume's own words:

After a repetition of similar instances, the mind is carried by habit, upon the appearance of an event, to expect its usual attendant, and to believe that it will exist. This connexion, therefore, which we feel in the mind, this customary transition of the imagination from one object to its usual attendant, is the sentiment or impression from which we form the idea of power or necessary connexion. Nothing farther is the case. Contemplate the subject on all sides; you will never find any other origin of that idea.

(Hume 1975: 75)

There are difficulties with this, however. Hume says that the only new thing that occurs after the repeated observation of B's following A's is that the mind is carried by habit, upon the appearance of one event to expect its usual attendant. What he means is that having repeatedly observed B's following A's we are caused by the next observation of an A to expect a B. That is, the complex mental event an observed constant conjunction of A's with B's + an impression of an A causes a belief in a B to occur. But that is not all. In addition a feeling is produced, and this is the sentiment or impression from which we form the idea of power or necessary connexion.

But what is this feeling? It is not the mere transition of the mind from one idea to another. Nor is it an impression of a necessary connection obtaining between the complex cause event: observing a constant conjunction of A's and B's + perceiving an A and the effect event: believing in the imminent occurrence of (forming a lively idea of) a B. For Hume's thesis is that a necessary connection is never observable between distinct events, whether mental or physical, since no two distinct events are necessarily connected.

In fact, Hume is insistent that we can no more get the idea of necessary connection by observing causal linkages in the mental realm than we can get it by observing causal linkages in the physical realm (Hume 1975: 64–9). The sentiment or impression Hume refers to can, therefore, only be an accompaniment to the transition from the idea of an A to the idea of a B, perhaps a feeling of helplessness or inevitability that occurs in the mind when the disposition to make the transition from an idea of an A to the idea of a B is activated. It is, therefore, only a contingent fact that it occurs when such a transition takes place since anything can cause anything and anything can fail to cause anything – a feature of it which Hume disguises from himself by his language, which consistently makes the impossible identification of the impression of necessary connection with 'the customary transition of the imagination' (Hume 1975: 75) or the 'propensity, which custom produces, to pass from an object to the idea of its usual attendant' (Hume 1978: 165).

The idea of necessity, then, has its origin in an impression of reflection, and so '[u]pon the whole, necessity is something, that exists in the mind, not in objects; nor is it possible for us ever to form the most distant idea of it, considered as a quality in bodies' (Hume 1978: 165–6).

Hume sums up in the Abstract: 'upon the whole, then, either we have no idea at all of force or energy, and these words are altogether insignificant, or they can mean nothing but that determination of the thought, acquired by habit, to pass from the cause to its usual effect'.

But we ascribe necessity to objects nonetheless. Hence Hume still has to explain this mistake.

Once again he does so by appealing to a general property of the human mind – the propensity of the mind 'to spread itself on external objects, and to conjoin with them any internal impressions, which they occasion, and which always make their appearances at the same time that these objects discover themselves to the senses' (Hume 1978: 167), 'for nothing is more usual than to apply to external objects every internal sensation, which they occasion' (Hume 1975: 78).

Hume merely notes this propensity in a footnote in the *Enquiry*, but in the more extended discussion of the *Treatise* he appeals to it at two other places. In section V of Part IV he appeals to it to explain our belief that tastes and smells, which have no spatial location, are located in the same place as visible and extended objects.

The explanation of this is the following:

> Tho' an extended object be incapable of a conjunction in place with another, that exists without any place or extension, yet they are susceptible of many other relations. Thus the taste and smell of any fruit are inseparable from its other qualities of colour and tangibility; and whichever of them be the cause or effect, 'tis certain they are always co-existent ... [and] ... co-temporary in their appearance in the mind; and 'tis upon the application of the extended body to our senses we perceive its particular taste and smell. These relations, then, of causation, and contiguity in the time of their appearance, betwixt the extended object and the quality, which exists without any particular place, ... have such an effect on the mind, that upon the appearance of one it will immediately turn its thought to the conception of the other ... [and] ... endeavour to give them a new relation, viz. that of a conjunction in place, that we may render the transition more easy and natural. For 'tis a quality ... in human nature ... that when objects are united by any relation, we have a strong propensity to add some new relation to them, in order to compleat the union.

(Hume 1978: 237)

Hume appeals to the same propensity to explain why the (Lockean) philosophers who distinguish external objects from their perceptions believe that the particular external objects resemble the perceptions they cause – because they add the relation of resemblance to that of causation 'to compleat the union' (Hume 1978: 217), and we can now see how it enables him likewise to explain our 'spreading the mind on the world' in the case of necessary connection. For here, just as in the case of tastes, the internal impression of reflection, which gives rise to the idea of necessity, is caused by the external situation, and contiguous in the time of its appearance. We therefore add the relation of conjunction in place to complete the union and render the transition more natural, that is, we ascribe an external spatial location between the objects to the necessary connection we have an idea of, though in doing so, as in the case of tastes, we are ascribing a location to something that really exists nowhere.

Later in the *Treatise*, and elsewhere in Hume's writings, the propensity to 'spread our mind on the world' is also invoked by Hume to explain our ascriptions of moral and aesthetic qualities to things.

This propensity is thus a very important one for Hume, but it is not easy to understand or to give uncontroversial examples.

What might seem a good example is given by A. H. Basson:

A clear case of projection occurred during the last war, when people wrote to the newspapers complaining of the gloomy and despondent note put forth by air raid sirens. Why they asked, could not the authorities have arranged for these to play some cheerful and encouraging tune, like 'Britannia Rules the Waves'? ... of course, ... the note of the sirens was not despondent or alarming, but its acquired associations induced despondency in the listener ... The projection was, in fact, nearly complete for most people: the warning note was actually felt as menacing, and the note at the end of the raid really sounded cheerful. But it could have been the other way round, and so we are intellectually convinced that the warning note was not in itself menacing, although it became impossible to imagine or to feel it as otherwise.

(Basson 1958: 66–7)

The writers to the newspapers thought not merely that the note made by the siren produced feelings of despondency, but also that it would have done so even in peacetime circumstances. So they thought that the note had a certain dispositional property: being such as to produce certain effects in human hearers. And their mistake (if mistake it was) was in thinking that this dispositional property was possessed by the note independently of its association with wartime circumstances. But, of course, the note could have had such an unconditional dispositional property. Thus, it might have been that the authorities had chosen as a warning note a sound that would have produced feelings of despondency in any normal human being, even in the most euphoric circumstance.

If our mistake, then, in 'spreading our minds on the world' and ascribing a necessary connection to causes and effects themselves, is analogous to the mistake made by Basson's writers to the newspapers, our belief in such a necessary connection in the objects, though false, will only be contingently false.

Now, of course, we can make such mistakes about the dispositions of external objects to affect human beings: finding something disgusting or boring, I might naively think that everyone will so do, that is, that the object has a disposition to produce that effect in every human being. And, if I discover that its power is less general than I supposed, all I will learn, like Basson's newspaper writers, if they were ever persuaded of their mistake, is that as a matter of fact, my original belief, though possibly true, was, in fact, mistaken.

Similarly, given that there is an impression of necessary connection which is produced in one's mind in the circumstances Hume supposes it would be possible to think that that impression of reflection had a less complex cause. And this mistake would be parallel to the mistake made by Basson's writers.

But this is not the mistake Hume intends when he speaks of 'spreading our minds on the world'. For this mistaken belief could have been true. For Hume, however, the ascription of necessity to objects is as absurd as the ascription of spatial location to smells and tastes. The latter involves 'such confusion and obscurity' that 'in our most familiar way of thinking' we:

[S]uppose that the taste exists within the circumference of the body, but in such a manner, that it fills the whole without extension, and exists entirely in each part without separation ... which is much the same as if we should say, that a thing is in a certain place and yet is not there.

(Hume 1978: 238)

Ascription of necessity to objects is similarly incoherent. For, recall: 'Upon the whole, necessity is something, that exists in the mind, not in objects; nor is it possible for us ever to form the most distant idea of it, considered as a quality in bodies' (Hume 1978: 165–6).

What Hume has in mind, in talking about the mind's spreading itself on the world, is something more like what we might call (following Shoemaker 1994: 295) literal projectivism. This is what would have been involved if Basson's writers had thought, not that the note of the siren would have produced despondent feelings in human beings even in peacetime, but that the note was itself feeling despondent.

Of course, this is not an intelligible thought, because the object in question could not possibly possess the property ascribed. But the same is true, Hume wants to say, of necessity considered as a quality in bodies: 'Either we have no idea of necessity, or necessity is nothing but the determination of the thought to pass from causes to effects and from effects to causes, according to their experienced union' (Hume 1978: 166).

However, the comparison with literal projectivism is not the most illuminating way to understand Hume's position, as we can see by looking more closely at his discussion of our propensity to ascribe a spatial location to tastes and smells. Our final state of 'confusion and obscurity' is the result of a three-stage process. First, via the propensity to 'compleat the union' by ascribing a new relation to objects already perceived as related by causation and contiguity in time, we come to think of the taste of the fig, say, as located within the boundaries of the fig. Second, however, reflection makes it clear that this is 'unintelligible and contradictory'.

Thus, influenced by two principles, our inclination to ascribe to the taste a location within the object, and our reason, which reveals this to be contradictory, we renounce neither principle, but as a last resort, involve the matter in confusion and obscurity to disguise the opposition from ourselves. The same three-stage process is involved in the origin of our belief (or rather, the ancient philosophers' belief) in substance and our belief in an enduring self, as we shall see later. The mechanism underlying it is that of the narrow imagination Hume opposes to reason and ascribes in the section 'Of the modern philosophy' to weak minds.

Thus our belief in a necessary connection between causes and effects is similarly best seen, on Hume's account, as the result of the narrow imagination's attempt to reconcile two irreconcilable principles. We know that literal projectivism is an error, that is, that the internal impression of necessity cannot be located in the objects, but we still cannot resist the propensity to 'spread our minds' on the world. But there are no genuine thoughts we can achieve by this means, anymore than there are genuine thoughts about substance or an enduring self. There are thoughts about what events in the world are constantly conjoined with other events in the world, and thoughts about what events in the world are constantly conjoined with others in the mind. In addition there is only 'confusion and obscurity' (Hume 1978: 238).

We can now turn to Hume's explicit definitions of causation.

Notoriously, Hume defines causation twice – as a philosophical relation: 'We may define a CAUSE to be an object precedent and contiguous to another, and where all the objects resembling the former are plac'd in like relations of precedency and contiguity to those objects that resemble the latter' (Hume 1978: 170, see also 1975: 76); and as a natural relation: 'A CAUSE is an object precedent and contiguous to another, and so united with it, that the idea of the one determines the mind to form the idea of the other, and the impression of the one to form a more lively idea of the other' (Hume 1978: 170, see also 1975: 77).

These two definitions are not equivalent, and neither one implies the other, and yet Hume puts them forward as giving two views of the same object. How can this be? The problem is not just that the two definitions assign different meanings to the term 'cause'. The problem is that they are not even extensionally equivalent: there are objects in the world which are causes according to the first definition, but not according to the second definition, and conversely.

Nevertheless, it seems clear enough what is going on, and that the problem of the inequivalent definitions poses no real problem for understanding Hume. According to Hume there are two things to be taken into account in explaining causation. There is what is going on in the world, independently of its effect on any observer. And there is what goes on in the mind of an observer who is prompted to apply the concept of causation to the world. Hume, as we have noted, in fact refers to his two definitions of causation as giving 'two views of the same object' and we can understand this metaphor in the light of the foregoing. The view of the object provided by the definition of cause as a philosophical relation is a view of it as it is in itself, independently of its effect on any possible observer. The view of the object presented by the definition of cause as a natural relation is a view of it in its role as something that affects the mind in a certain way.

However, we can now see that there is another apparent objection to Hume's procedure. This is the objection that the second definition is circular: it defines causation in terms of itself. For it results in a cause being defined as something the idea of which in a suitable mind would cause certain changes to take place.

The only response a defender of Hume can give to this objection is to acknowledge that the second definition would be circular if taken by itself, but insist that it is not to be taken by itself. It must be paired with the first definition. Hence the causal verb 'determines' in the second definition of 'cause' can be understood in terms of the first definition and the circularity eliminated.

Of course, this means that Hume's metaphor of 'two views of the same object' is inappropriate: the second definition can no longer be thought of as giving us a way of thinking about causation which is independent of the way of thinking of causation given us by the first definition.

Given the fanfare with which Hume announced the search for the origin of the idea of necessary connection, another disadvantage of interpreting his second definition in terms of his first might also seem to be that by doing so we unfortunately eliminate any trace of a reference to necessity or necessary connection in Hume's final account of causation.

A possible response to this is that the verb 'determines' in the second definition can be understood as containing a reference to the impression of reflection that is produced, along with the transition from the idea of the cause to the idea of the effect, when a constant conjunction is observed. And this element of the second definition need not be deleted if the first definition is applied to eliminate the circularity.

However this may be, the most important point to note is that even if the second definition is read in such a way as to bring the idea of necessary connection into the account, it will still not have the role Hume wishes for it, that is, the role of an idea of something 'the mind spreads on the world'. For the judgement that something is a cause according to the second definition, like the judgement that it is a cause according to the first definition, could be true. But as we have seen, if I 'spread my mind on the world' I do not think a possibly true thought.

There is another way in which the idea of necessary connection is unsuited to Hume's purpose, which Stroud (1977) emphasizes:

> We have seen that the impression of necessity Hume claims to find has to be thought of as an impression of reflection that accompanies the transition from the idea of the cause to the idea of the effect. But such accompaniment must be contingent. There could be creatures in which the transition was made without it. They would, according to Hume's theory, lack any idea of necessity at all. But they could make all the transitions in thought we do, form lively ideas (beliefs) just as we do, and in general engage in all the activities of life just as we do.
>
> Stroud (1977: 227)

Thus it appears that the idea of necessary connection, on Hume's account, is a redundant addition to our stock of mental ideas, something which need have no reflection in the inferences we make, the beliefs we hold etc. Of course, this is not what Hume intends, and his language, in which the impossible identification of the impression of necessary connection with the transition from the perception of the cause to the idea of the effect is constantly suggested, indicates his implicit awareness of the unsatisfactoriness of this position. Nevertheless, the epiphenomenal character of the idea of necessary connection is unavoidable within his theory. Just because the story Hume tells is itself through and through causal and so deals in contingencies, it cannot account for our idea of causation satisfactorily if that idea is assumed to involve, as an essential element, an idea of necessary connection.

Chapter Four

The external world

The continued and distinct existence of body

In Part IV of Book I of the *Treatise* Hume turns to an examination of 'the sceptical and other systems of philosophy'. As argued in the last chapter, it is in this Part of the *Treatise*, rather than in the more celebrated discussions of causation and induction in Part III, that Hume's own scepticism emerges. In the first section of Part IV, 'Of scepticism with regard to reason', Hume first presents what he takes to be a *sound* argument that (a) all knowledge (in the strict sense which he uses for the product of demonstrative reasoning) degenerates to probability and (b) all probability reduces to zero, so that 'all the rules of logic require a continual diminution, and at last a total extinction of belief and evidence' (1978: 182). However, he argues, though if we thus follow the dictates of reason consistently all belief will be eliminated, in fact we will continue to believe. For: 'Nature, by an absolute and uncontrollable necessity has determin'd us to judge as well as to breathe and feel' (1978: 183).

The argument by which Hume thinks it can be shown that 'the rules of logic require a total extinction of belief and evidence' is generally acknowledged by commentators to be fallacious, but its main significance lies in what it shows about Hume's attitude to scepticism. Hume returns to the topic in the final section of Part IV. However, for our purposes section I is of relevance for the way in which Hume thinks it leads on to section II, 'Of scepticism with regard to the senses', in which he turns to the topic of our belief in an external world. In both cases, Hume thinks, it is not reason that accounts for belief but human nature:

> Thus the sceptic still continues to reason and believe, even tho' he asserts that he cannot defend his reason by reason; and by the same rule he must assent to the principle concerning the existence of body, tho' he cannot pretend by any arguments of philosophy to maintain its veracity. Nature has not left this to his choice.

> (1978: 187)

Thus Hume's aim in his discussion is not to explore whether we are justified in our belief in an external world, or to raise the sceptical question whether an external world exists. He writes, 'we may well ask, *what causes induce us to believe in the existence of body?* But 'tis in vain to ask, *whether there be body or not?* That is a point, which we must take for granted in all our reasonings' (1978: 187).

Right at the outset of his discussion then, Hume limits his enquiry to the causes of our belief in an external world, emphasizing that this is the only question we can sensibly ask. However, this should not lead us to think that Hume's subsequent discussion will be neutral with respect to the question whether an external world exists, or whether we are justified in believing that it does. On the contrary, the course of Hume's subsequent discussion is profoundly sceptical. He distinguishes two versions of the belief in an external world – the version of the vulgar and the version of the philosopher. He then gives an account of the belief in its vulgar form that exhibits it as *false*. But the belief in its philosophical form, Hume argues, is no better: in fact, it is merely a fallback position to which philosophers necessarily retreat when they realize that the vulgar form of the belief, which is its natural form, is untenable; it has no *primary* recommendation to reason or imagination (not even to the narrow imagination), but acquires all its force from the vulgar form; it is the 'monstrous offspring of two principles which are contrary to each other' (1978: 215) and what is worse (as emerges finally, not in Section II, but in Section IV, 'Of the modern philosophy'), it too is false, or, more carefully, can be shown to be false by an argument that 'will appear entirely conclusive to every one that comprehends it' (1978: 229).

Hume begins his account of the causes of our belief in an external world, or our belief 'in body', as he puts it, by distinguishing two elements within that belief. First there is the belief that objects *continue* to exist even when they are not 'present to the senses', and second, there is the belief that they have an existence *distinct* from the mind and perception and are capable of existing *independently* of and *external* to us (1978: 188).

The first of these beliefs, Hume notes, entails the second. For, of course, what *is* so *can* be so: 'if the objects of our senses continue to exist, even when they are not perceiv'd, their existence is, of course, independent of and distinct from the perception' (1978: 188). And Hume goes on to add, without explanation, that the second belief entails the first, which it does not (1978: 188). But, he says, even though

> [T]he decision of the one question decides the other; yet that we may the more easily discover the principles of human nature, from whence the decision arises, we shall carry along with us this distinction, and shall consider, whether it be the *senses, reason,* or the *imagination* that produces the opinion of a *continu'd* or of a *distinct* existence.
>
> (1978: 188)

Of course, Hume's conclusion is that it is the third of these possible causes, imagination, which produces our belief in body, and it does so, he thinks, primarily by producing a belief in a *continued* existence.

The vulgar and philosophical forms of the belief in body

In order to understand Hume's discussion, however, it is necessary first to attend to the distinction he makes between the vulgar and philosophical forms of the belief in body. For, though Hume thinks that neither is intellectually defensible, they arise in significantly different ways, and in a definite sequence.

To appreciate Hume's distinction recall that Hume *reifies* perceptions. As we know, according to Hume any mental activity involves the presence before the mind of perceptions. And, for Hume, these perceptions are *things* to which the mind stands in the relation of *perceiving*. Moreover, there is no logical absurdity in supposing that these things, though in fact perceived, might exist *unperceived*: 'the name of *perception* renders not this separation from mind absurd and contradictory' (1978: 207). That is, though perceptions are so called because they are perceived, the objects so called can exist unperceived.

We can now explain the distinction between the vulgar and the philosophical forms of the belief in an external world. Hume thinks that, according to the vulgar, their perceptions *do* continue to exist unperceived. Thus they have a *continued* existence and are *distinct* from and *independent* of perception. According to the vulgar, moreover, nothing else has such a continued and distinct existence; thus perceptions comprise the furniture of the world. According to the philosophical form of the belief in an external world, by contrast, (in speaking of which Hume mainly has Locke in mind) this is not so. Perceptions do not exist unperceived. However, there are *other* objects, distinct from perceptions, which do, and, in fact, never are perceived, but cause in us the perceptions that we do perceive. These unperceived causes of perceptions, Hume thinks, must be allowed by the philosophers to be similar to perceptions: '[f]or as to the notion of external existence, when taken for something specifically different from our perceptions, we have already shewn its absurdity' (1978: 188). In fact, he thinks, they must be allowed to be 'in their nature ... exactly the same with perceptions' (1978: 218). Nevertheless, they are an *addition* to the ontology of the vulgar, a 'new set of perceptions' (1978: 218), acceptance of which is made necessary by the philosophers' denial that perceptions, properly speaking, have a continued or distinct existence. Hume thus calls this philosophical view a system of *double* existence.

Hume's aim then in section II is to explain how both the vulgar and the philosophers have come to believe in the existence of an external world. He denies that the belief in either form is the product of the senses or reason and argues that the imagination is responsible for both forms of the belief, directly for the vulgar form of the belief and indirectly for the philosophical form. Thus we should look in his discussion for six components:

1. An argument that the senses cannot be the cause of the vulgar form of the belief;
2. An argument that the senses cannot be the cause of the philosophical form of the belief;
3. An argument that reason cannot be the cause of the vulgar form of the belief;
4. An argument that reason cannot be the cause of the philosophical form of the belief;
5. An explanation of the way the imagination operates *directly* to produce the vulgar form of the belief; and
6. An explanation of the way the imagination operates *indirectly* to produce the philosophical form of the belief in an external world.

These six components are indeed present in his discussion, though the first four, in particular, are not always clearly distinguished.

First, Hume asks whether the senses can produce the belief in an external world. He dismisses, brusquely, the suggestion that the senses can give rise to a belief in a *continued* existence, for to do so they would have to 'operate, even after they have ceas'd all manner of operation' (1978: 188).

The best the senses could do, then, would be to produce a belief in *distinct* existence. But they cannot do this either, Hume argues. For to do so they must 'present their impressions ... as images and representations' (1978: 189) (if they are being thought of as producing the philosophical form of the belief in an external world), or 'as these very distinct and external existences' (if they are being thought of as producing the vulgar form of the belief in an external world).

The first possibility can be excluded, however, Hume argues. For the senses never convey anything but a single perception. When I look at a table I do not see *two* things – a perception and something it represents. Thus the senses cannot produce the belief in a 'double existence', which must be arrived at, therefore, 'by some inference of the reason or imagination' (1978: 189).

Hume next turns to the second possibility: that the senses present our perceptions as themselves being distinct existences. He distinguishes two components in the notion of a distinct existence: externality and independence. Externality is a spatial notion: x is external from y if and only if x is located apart from y. Independence is a modal notion: x is independent of y if and only if x could exist even if y did not, and x is independent of being acted on in a particular way by y if x could exist even if it were not acted on in that way by y.

We shall look at Hume's arguments that the senses do not and cannot produce a belief that our perceptions are themselves independent existences before looking at what he says about externality.

The first point he emphasizes is that if our senses do produce a belief that our perceptions are independent existents they operate by a 'kind of fallacy and illusion'. For, as a matter of empirically discoverable fact, our perceptions are not *independent* existences and the belief in an external world in its vulgar form is *false*.

But, Hume thinks, our senses cannot deceive us in this way. To suppose that they can is to suppose that, whilst *none* of our perceptions have the modal property of being capable of existing independently of being perceived, some appear to us to do so, and others do not appear to us to do so. However, this is not so:

> [E]very impression, external and internal, passions, affections, sensations, pains and pleasures, are originally on the same footing, and ... whatever other differences we may observe among them, they appear, all of them, in their true colours, as impressions or perceptions ... nor is it conceivable that our senses shou'd be more capable of deceiving us in the situation and relations, than in the nature of our impressions. For since all actions and sensations of the mind are known to us by consciousness, they must necessarily

appear in every particular what they are, and be what they appear. Everything that enters the mind, being in *reality* a perception, 'tis impossible any thing shou'd to *feeling* appear different. This were to suppose, that even where we are most intimately conscious we might be mistaken.

(Hume 1978: 190)

This insistence on the incorrigibility of our beliefs about what we 'are most intimately conscious' of is unsatisfying. But recall the precise nature of the proposition that Hume is trying to refute: that some, though not all, of our perceptions present themselves to us as possessors of a modal property that they do not possess – being independent of our perception. Hume, in fact, is more convincing three paragraphs later, when he denies outright that this property could ever be an object of the senses, whether or not our perceptions have it. For we can perceive what things are, but not what they *are not but could be*: 'As to the independency of our perceptions on ourselves, this can never be an object of the senses, but any opinion we form concerning it must be derived from experience and observation' (Hume 1978: 191).

Anyway, even if our senses could deceive us, we could only get from them the idea of perceptions as distinct existences if we could perceive, not only the perceptions, but also ourselves. For distinctness is a relation and to be aware of a relation we must also be aware of its relata: 'Now if the senses presented our impressions as external to, and independent of ourselves, both the objects and ourselves must be obvious to our senses, otherwise they cou'd not be compar'd by these faculties' (Hume 1978: 189).

But, Hume argues, that we do not perceive ourselves is evident from the difficulty of the problem of personal identity. (Really, what lies behind Hume's confidence here is his yet to be explained *solution* to the problem of personal identity, which involves the contention that there is no *impression* of self at all.)

These, then, in sketchy outline, are Hume's arguments against the claim that the senses give us our belief in a world of independently existing objects. To simplify the exposition I have left out Hume's discussion of the question of *external* existence, and I must now explain why.

Briefly put, the point is that externality is a spatial notion and the only intelligible sense that can be given to the claim that an object is external is that it is external to one's body. However, human bodies are *part* of the 'external world' discussed by philosophers. Hence an explanation of the belief 'in body', i.e. in an external world, in the philosophically interesting sense, cannot just take the form of an explanation of our belief in the spatial externality of objects, for that is to presuppose an already existing 'external world'. Hume makes this point himself, albeit in a somewhat unfortunate phrasing which presupposes the doctrine of 'double existence' (Hume 1978: 191).

Hume sums up his discussion of the role of the senses in the following way:

> [T]hey give us no notion of continu'd existence, because they cannot operate beyond the extent, in which they really operate. They as little produce the opinion of a distinct existence, because they can neither offer it to the mind as represented nor as original. To offer it as represented, they must present both an object and an image. To make it appear as original, they must convey a falsehood ... In order to which they must be able to compare the object with ourselves; and even in that case they do not, nor is it possible they shou'd, deceive us. We may, therefore, conclude ... that the opinion of a continu'd and of a distinct existence never arises from the senses.

> (Hume 1978: 191–2)

However, he does not leave the matter there, but returns to the claim that all our perceptions appear as they are, dependent and interrupted beings. There are, he says, three classes of impressions conveyed by the senses: those of the primary qualities, figure, bulk, motion and solidity; those of the secondary qualities, colour, smells, tastes, sounds, heat and cold; and those of the pains and pleasures arising from the application of objects to our bodies. All of these appear to our senses 'on the same footing' in the manner of their existence, that is, as dependent and interrupted, but neither the vulgar nor philosophers acknowledge this. According to the vulgar, secondary qualities are on a par with primary qualities, Hume says, as present in the objects themselves, and therefore not 'on the same footing' as pleasures and pains. Whilst, according to the philosophers, secondary qualities are on a par with pleasures and pains, as not representations of anything really present in objects, and not 'on a footing' with primary qualities. Thus neither the vulgar form of the belief in an external world nor the philosophical form can be a product of the senses, but must arise from reason or the imagination.

The claim of reason to be the origin of our belief in an external world is dealt with more briefly. Hume again distinguishes the two versions of the belief, and first considers the claim of reason to be the origin of the vulgar man's belief.

He dismisses it on two grounds. First, to claim that reason is the source of the belief is to claim that it is based on *argument*, but 'whatever convincing arguments philosophers may fancy they can produce ... 'tis obvious ... 'tis not by them, that children, peasants, and the greatest part of mankind are induc'd to attribute objects to some impressions, and deny them to others' (Hume 1978: 193).

Moreover, Hume claims, reason cannot be the source of the vulgar man's belief, because the vulgar man's belief is *false*, 'For philosophy informs us, that everything, which appears to the mind, is nothing but a perception and is interrupted and dependent on the mind' (Hume 1978: 193).

Hume's argument against the contention that the philosopher's belief in an external world is due to reason is not given at this point, but its character is indicated: 'Even after we distinguish our perceptions from our objects, 'twill appear presently, that we are still incapable of reasoning from the existence of one to that of the other' (Hume 1978: 193).

And the promised argument appears nineteen pages later, as a demonstration that 'this philosophical hypothesis has no primary recommendation ... to reason' (Hume 1978: 212):

The only conclusion we can draw from the existence of one thing to that of another, is by means of the relation of cause and effect ... The idea of this relation is derived from past experience, by which we find, that two beings are constantly conjoined together, and are always present at once to the mind. But as no beings are ever present to the mind but perceptions ... we may observe a conjunction

> ... between different perceptions, but can never observe it between
> perceptions and objects. 'Tis impossible, therefore, that from the
> existence or any of the qualities of the former, we can ever form any
> conclusion concerning the existence of the latter.
>
> (Hume 1978: 212)

Hume is thus left with the imagination as the only possible source
of the 'entirely unreasonable' (Hume 1978: 193) belief in body.
And since he believes that the philosophical system has no primary recommendation to the imagination his approach is first to
explain how the imagination can give rise to the vulgar form of the
belief. He is, therefore, faced with two tasks: to explain how the
imagination can create the idea of perceptions with a 'continu'd
and distinct' existence, and to explain how belief can reside in 'so
extraordinary an opinion' (Hume 1978: 195).

The causes of the vulgar form of the belief in body: constancy and coherence

Since it is the belief in body in its vulgar form with which Hume is
concerned, he takes it that his task is to identify qualities of perceptions which, acting on the imagination, cause it to generate the
belief that they have a 'continu'd and distinct' existence. These
qualities of perceptions, in concurrence with certain qualities of
the imagination, will play the same role in relation to the generation of our belief in an external world that constant conjunction,
in concurrence with the imagination's propensity to spread itself
on external objects, plays in relation to the generation of our belief
in a necessary connection between causes and effects.

The first qualities of perceptions he notices are the involun-
tariness of certain perceptions and their superior force and
violence. But he notices these only to dismiss them, for he points
out that bodily pains and pleasures possess these qualities also, but
we do not regard them as having a continued and distinct existence (Hume 1978: 194).

The crucial qualities of perceptions, in the present connection,
Hume claims, are rather their *constancy* and *coherence.*

In fact, these are qualities of series of perceptions, rather than of perceptions taken singly. A constant series of perceptions is just one, all of whose members are exactly alike. Thus, if I look at a mountain and then shut my eyes or turn my head, the mountain will look exactly the same when I see it again – the sequence of my perceptions of it will thus be constant, albeit gappy. Coherence is a slightly more complicated notion: a series of perceptions is coherent if it is orderly, that is, if it exhibits a pattern that other series of perceptions also exhibit. Thus, Hume writes,

> [W]hen I return to my chamber after an hour's absence, I find not my fire in the same situation in which I left it: But then I am accustomed in other instances to see a like alteration produced in a like time ... This coherence, therefore, in their changes is one of the characteristics of external objects.
>
> (Hume 1978: 195)

Hume spends a considerable amount of time discussing the role of coherence and elaborates its role in producing the belief in continued and distinct existence in a way that suggests it is merely an extension of our customary causal reasoning. He illustrates this with an example of a porter delivering a letter:

> I hear ... a noise as of a door turning upon its hinges, and a little later see a porter ... I have never observ'd that this noise cou'd proceed from anything but the motion of a door; and therefore conclude, that the present phenomenon is a contradiction to all past experience, unless the door ... be still in being ... I receive a letter ... from a friend, who says he is two hundred leagues distant ... I can never account for this phenomenon, conformable to my experience in other instances, without spreading out in my mind the whole sea and continent between us ... To consider these phenomena of the porter and letter in a certain light, they are contradictions to common experience, and ... objections to those maxims, which we form concerning ... causes and effects. I am accustom'd to hear such a sound and see such an object in motion at the same time. I have not receiv'd in this particular instance both these perceptions. These observations are contrary, unless I suppose that the door still remains, and that it was open'd without my perceiving it.
>
> (Hume 1978: 196–7)

Despite the attention to detail in this illustration, however, Hume does not, in fact, wish to say that 'this conclusion from the coherence of appearances' is 'of the same nature as' our reasonings concerning cause and effect. He maintains that the two are considerably different, and that the inference from coherence 'arises from the understanding and from custom in an indirect and oblique manner' (Hume 1978: 197). The last phrase is an allusion to his previous discussion in section XII of cases of causal inference in which we are not presented with constant conjunctions but a contrariety of effects (Hume 1978: 133), as when twenty ships go out to sea but I observe only nineteen to return (Hume 1978: 134). Hume thinks that in such cases the belief that will be formed on the basis of past experience will be less firm and solid than that formed on the basis of an observed constant conjunction, and his chief reservation about coherence appears to be that the belief we form in an external world is *too* firm and solid to be based on the limited and contradictory evidence which he views as its basis: 'Any degree ... of regularity in our perceptions, can never be a foundation for us to infer a greater degree of regularity in some objects, which are not perceiv'd, since this supposes a contradiction, *viz.* a habit acquired by what was never present to the mind' (Hume 1978: 197).

Thus, he thinks, in this case, 'the extending of custom and reasoning beyond the perceptions can never be the direct and natural effect of the constant repetition and connexion' (Hume 1978: 198), but must arise from the co-operation of some other principle.

The principle he resorts to he expresses metaphorically: 'the imagination, when set into any train of thinking, is apt to continue, even when its object fails it, and like a galley put in motion by the oars, carries on its course without any new impulse' (Hume 1978: 198). But, without explaining why, Hume insists that this principle is 'too weak to support alone so vast an edifice as is that of the continu'd existence of all external bodies; and that we must join the *constancy* of their appearance to the *coherence*, in order to give a satisfactory account of that opinion' (Hume 1978: 198–9).

He summarizes the role of constancy as follows (Hume 1978: 199). The perception of the sun or the ocean is sometimes interrupted, but it often returns to us exactly as it was before, i.e. it looks exactly the same each time I look at it. It is, therefore, natural for us to think of the interrupted perceptions not as different (which they really are), but on the contrary, to regard them as individually the same, on account of their resemblance. But we are also aware of the interruption and see that it is contrary to the 'perfect identity' of the different perceptions. The mind is thus pulled in two directions and involved in a kind of contradiction. We resolve the conflict by supposing that the interrupted perceptions are joined by a real existence of which we are insensible, that is, that they continue to exist unperceived. This supposition derives vivacity from the memory of the interrupted perceptions and the propensity that they give us to suppose them the same. Having this lively idea of their continued existence, given Hume's account of belief, *is* to believe in their continued existence. Thus the vulgar belief in an external world is explained as an erroneous product of the natural working of the imagination.

The role of identity

Having summarized in this way his account of the origin of the vulgar man's false belief, Hume turns to a more detailed analysis of the mechanism of its genesis, which he refers to as his 'system'. There are, he says, four tasks to be carried out. First, to explain the *principium individuationis*, or principle of identity. Second, to explain 'why the resemblance of our broken and interrupted perceptions induces us to attribute an identity to them' (Hume 1978: 200). Third, to account for the propensity, which this illusion gives, to unite their broken appearances by a continued existence. Fourth and lastly, to explain the force and vivacity of conception, which arises from the propensity and constitutes belief.

Hume begins his account of identity by posing a dilemma:

[T]he view of any one object is not sufficient to convey the idea of identity. For in that proposition *an object is the same with itself*, if the idea expressed by the word, *object*, were no ways distinguished

> from that [one] meant by *itself*, we really should mean nothing ...
> One single object conveys the idea of unity, not that of identity. On
> the other hand, a multiplicity of objects can never convey this idea,
> however resembling they may be supposed.

(Hume 1978: 200)

Hume's puzzle is due to the fact that identity is a *relation*, but a
relation a thing can have *only to itself*. The perception of one object,
he thinks, can never give us the idea of a relation; on the other hand,
the perception of more than one object can never give us the idea of
a relation a thing can have only to itself. If ideas are thought of, as in
Hume, as images, his puzzlement is easy to appreciate.

Thus, Hume professes himself baffled: 'Since ... both number
and unity are incompatible with the relation of identity, it must lie
in ... neither of them. But to tell the truth, at first sight this seems
utterly impossible. Betwixt unity and number there can be no
medium' (Hume 1978: 200).

To solve this problem Hume has recourse to the idea of time or
duration. Earlier in the *Treatise* he has argued that time implies
succession, i.e. change, and that the idea of time or duration is
not applicable in a proper sense to unchanging objects (Hume
1978: 37).

When we think of an unchanging object as having duration,
then, this is only by a 'fiction of the imagination', by which 'the
unchangeable [sic] object is suppos'd to participate of the changes
of the co-existing objects and in particular that of our perceptions'(Hume 1978: 20). The unchanging object does *not* endure,
strictly speaking, but this 'fiction of the imagination almost universally takes place'; and it is by means of it, Hume thinks, that we
get the idea of identity. Suppose we are gazing at the wall, on which
hangs a picture of David Hume and a clock with a second hand.
The picture is an unchanging object, which reveals no interruption or variation and, therefore, considered in isolation, will yield
the idea of unity but not that of time or duration. If the picture
were *all* we were surveying and if nothing else were going on in
our minds then it would be as if no time had passed. But we can
also see the clock. In consequence, as well as the unchanging

sequence of perceptions of the picture there is also the changing sequence of perceptions of the clock. This second sequence, which answers to our idea of number, gives us the idea of time, which genuinely applies to it. And now, Hume suggests, when we survey these two sequences together we suppose the unchanging sequence to participate in the changes of the changing sequence and thus imagine *it* to have genuine duration. Thus we arrive at the idea of identity, viz. 'the invariableness and uninterruptedness of any object, thro' a suppos'd variation of time'. Here, then, Hume triumphantly concludes, 'is an idea which is a medium betwixt unity and number or more properly speaking, is either of them, according to the view in which we take it: And this idea we call that of identity' (Hume 1978: 201).

Although this is hardly clear, or even coherent, one point at least emerges fairly evidently. Namely, that it cannot just be to *variable* or *interrupted* objects, in Hume's view, that the idea of identity must be inapplicable: the same must be true of invariable and uninterrupted objects. The idea of identity, to be distinct from the idea of unity, must imply duration, but duration implies change. Even the paradigm from which we get the idea of identity, then, must be a case to which it does not apply. For the notion of an object existing through a period of time without change is a contradiction in terms.

If this is right the reason Hume gives for the inapplicability of the notion of identity to the perceptions in a constant series, namely their brokenness and interruptedness, is misleading, or at least superfluous: given his analysis of the notion of identity there is *nothing* it is applicable to. However, the radical scepticism to which this line of thought would lead is not addressed by Hume: he is content to insist that identity is, at least, incompatible with change or interruption and with this conclusion in hand he proceeds to the next stage in the construction of his system.

His second task was to explain why the constancy of our perceptions leads us to ascribe to them a perfect numerical identity, despite their interruptedness.

Hume summarizes his account of this as follows. In contemplating an identical, i.e. an invariable and unchanging, object, we are doing something very different from contemplating a succession of objects related by links of resemblance, as in a constant sequence, but:

> That action of the imagination, by which we consider the uninterrupted ... object, and that by which we reflect on the succession of related objects, are almost the same to the feeling, nor is there much more effort of thought required in the latter case than in the former. The relation facilitates the transmission of the mind from one object to another, and renders its passage as smooth as if it contemplated one continu'd object. This resemblance is the cause of the confusion and mistake, and makes us substitute the notion of identity, instead of that of related objects. However at one instant we may consider the related succession as variable or interrupted, we are sure the next to ascribe to it a perfect identity, and regard it as invariable and uninterrupted.
>
> (Hume 1978: 253–4)

Stripped to its bare essentials the mechanism Hume refers to here is supposed to operate as follows to generate the belief that the members of a constant series of perceptions are identical. I often have impressions which seem to remain invariable and uninterrupted over a stretch of time – as when I gaze for ten minutes at a picture of David Hume. This may be depicted thus:

(1) AAAAAAAAAA

I take this to be the contemplation of an identical, i.e. invariable and uninterrupted, object. But if I close my eyes or look away for a few seconds I will have an interrupted sequence of perceptions:

(2) AAAAXXXAAA.

However, in situation (2) there is 'the same uninterrupted passage of the imagination' (Hume 1978: 203) as in situation (1). Situation (2) places the mind in the same 'disposition and is considered with the same smooth and uninterrupted progress of the imagination, as attends the view of' (Hume 1978: 201) situation (1). But 'whatever ideas place the mind in the same disposition, or in similar ones, are apt to be confounded' (Hume 1978: 203). Thus I confound situation (2) with situation (1). But since I take situation (1) to be a view of an identical object I do the same with situation (2) and 'confound the succession with the identity' (Hume 1978: 204). This is Hume's account of the second element in his system.

The third element is now easy to account for. I could regard situation (2) as a view of a single identical object without thinking of any perceptions as having a continuous unobserved existence if I were willing to allow that objects could have a gappy existence. But Hume insists that it is an essential part of the notion of identity that an identical object must be *uninterrupted* as well as invariable in its existence. Thus, though I cannot fail to notice the apparent interruption in situation (2), consistently with maintaining that (2) *is* a view of an identical object, I cannot allow that there really is an interruption. Consequently, I unite the 'broken appearances' by means of 'the fiction of a continu'd existence' (Hume 1978: 205). That is, I come to believe that the identical *perception A* which I earlier perceived has continued in existence whilst I was not perceiving it and is now again being perceived by me. I come to the *belief* that this is so, and not merely to the *thought* that it is so, because – and this is the fourth element in Hume's system – the liveliness of the memory impressions is transmitted to the thought. This, then, in Hume's view is the form that the belief in body takes in the mind of the vulgar, i.e. the non-philosophers. They believe that their very perceptions have a continued and distinct existence.

The philosophical belief in double existence

Philosophers know better. *As a matter of empirically discoverable fact*, Hume thinks, perceptions are dependent and perishing existences. This, he thinks, is easily established by a few experiments familiar to philosophers.

> When we press one eye with a finger, we immediately perceive all the objects to become double ... But as we do not attribute a continu'd existence to both these perceptions, and as they are both of the same nature, we clearly perceive that all our perceptions, are

> dependent on our organs, and the disposition of our senses and animal spirits. This experiment is confirm'd ... by an infinite number of other experiments of the same kind; from all which we learn, that our sensible perceptions are not possest of any distinct or independent existence.

> (Hume 1978: 211)

But the psychological mechanism by which we confound situation (2) with situation (1) is too powerful even for philosophers to resist. They cannot help, any more than the vulgar, regarding situation (2) as a view of an identical object. However, they know that perceptions do not continue unperceived. To resolve their conflict all they can do is to distinguish between *objects* and *perceptions* ascribing the continuity and distinctness to the former, and the interruptedness to the latter. But such a system of 'double existence', Hume thinks, is only a 'palliative remedy' and 'contains all the difficulties of the vulgar system, with some others that are peculiar to itself' (Hume 1978: 211). Thus the psychological mechanism which leads us to confound situation (2) with situation (1) necessarily involves us, whether we are philosophers or the vulgar, in intellectual error.

There are two points Hume emphasizes about this system of 'double existence' in section II of Part IV. The first is that 'there are no principles either of the understanding or fancy, which lead us directly to embrace this opinion of the double existence of perceptions and objects' (Hume 1978: 211). The second is that we cannot 'arrive at it but by passing thro' the common hypothesis of the identity and continuance of our interrupted perceptions' (Hume 1978: 211). The first point Hume argues in two steps. First he argues that the understanding or reason can provide no possible justification for the philosophical system. We have already seen his argument for this. To attempt to infer anything about objects from the patterns presented in perception would be like attempting to infer facts about fires from facts about smoke patterns when only smoke patterns were ever perceived.

Second, Hume argues, the doctrine of double existence could not even be a *primary* product of the imagination or fancy, imagination in the narrow sense. Or rather, he declares himself unable to see how this could possibly be shown to be the case:

> Let it be taken for granted, that our perceptions are broken, and interrupted, and however like, are still different from each other; and let anyone upon this supposition shew why the fancy, directly and immediately, proceeds to the belief of another existence, resembling these perceptions in their nature, but yet continu'd, and uninterrupted and identical; and after he has done this to my satisfaction, I promise to renounce my present opinion.
>
> (Hume 1978: 212–13)

The natural view that recommends itself to the imagination, Hume argues, is the vulgar view, even though it is provably false. Thus, he concludes, the philosophical system is necessarily a *secondary product of the imagination.*

In section II this is all that Hume says about the philosophical view, but it is not all that he has to say about it because he returns to it in section IV, 'Of the modern philosophy' (whose argument is summarised again in the *Enquiry*). Here he argues, as we have seen already, that there is a necessary conflict between reason and the imagination. The philosophical view, along with the vulgar, can be seen, by the application of reason, to be false – though belief in an external world, in one form or other, is an unavoidable and irremovable product of the activities of the imagination.

His argument for this conclusion, briefly outlined earlier, rests on a consideration of the relation between primary and secondary qualities. Its target is the element common to the vulgar and philosophical forms of the belief in an external world, that there are objects which are independent of perception, which continue to exist unperceived, and *which possess additional qualities which entitle one to think of them as material objects.* As Hume expresses its conclusion: 'it is [not] possible for us to reason justly and regularly from causes and effects [the only kind of reasoning, remember, which can assure us of any matter of fact] and at the same time believe the continu'd existence of matter' Hume (1978: 266). This conclusion is repeated in the *Enquiry*: 'the opinion of *external* existence ... [is] contrary to reason' (Hume 1975: 155).

Clearly, the falsity of the belief in an external world does not follow from the fact that that belief is false in its vulgar form; nor does it follow from that fact, together with the fact that it is impossible to give any reason for the belief in its philosophical form. What more is needed is an argument that the properties which we take to be definitive of material objects are none of them possessed by any independent and continuous objects, but only, if at all, by perceptions. And this, in fact, is how Hume argues. He first argues that the *secondary* qualities can be possessed only by perceptions, and next that the *primary* qualities can only be possessed by something possessing secondary qualities. Hence, he concludes, neither type of property can be possessed by something independent and continuous, and so the belief in an external world, in either its vulgar or its philosophical form, must be rejected.

The statement of this argument in the *Enquiry* makes clear the overall structure:

> It is universally allowed by modern enquirers, that all the sensible qualities of objects, such as hard, soft, cold, hot, white, black, etc., are merely secondary, and exist not in the objects themselves, but are perceptions of the mind, without any external archetype or model, which they represent. If this be allowed, with regard to secondary qualities, it must also follow, with regard to the supposed primary qualities of extension and solidity; nor can the latter be any more entitled to that denomination than the former. The idea of extension is entirely acquired from the senses of sight and feeling; and if all the qualities perceived by the senses, be in the mind, not in the object, the same conclusion must reach the idea of extension, which is wholly dependent on the sensible ideas, or ideas of secondary qualities.

(Hume 1975: 254)

In this passage Hume does not give any argument for the proposition that secondary properties are only in the mind; he simply asserts it as universally agreed by modern enquirers. In the *Treatise*, however, he indicates which of the arguments of the modern philosophers he finds convincing, namely 'that deriv'd from the variations of those impressions, even while the external object, to all appearance continues the same' (Hume 1978: 226).

And, in fact, he indicates that he finds this argument 'as satisfactory as can possibly be imagined' (Hume 1978: 227).

But Hume goes beyond the modern philosophers in arguing that the same is true of primary qualities. He argues for this conclusion by arguing that only an object possessing secondary qualities can possess primary qualities, for we can form no idea of an object with primary qualities which possesses no secondary qualities. To establish this, Hume concentrates on the two primary qualities of extension and solidity. He argues that we cannot conceive of an extended object which *neither* possesses some secondary quality *nor* possesses solidity: 'tis impossible to conceive extension, but as compos'd of parts, endow'd with colour or solidity' (Hume 1978: 228). But 'colour is excluded from any real existence'. 'The reality, therefore, of our idea of extension depends upon the reality of that of solidity' (Hume 1978: 228). But the idea of solidity is the idea of 'two objects, which being impelled by the utmost force, cannot penetrate each other, but still maintain a separate and distinct existence' (Hume 1978: 228). Solidity, therefore, is incomprehensible alone, and without the conception of some bodies that are solid and maintain this separate and distinct existence. But what idea can we have of these bodies? We cannot think of them as possessing secondary qualities, nor extension, since extension without secondary qualities presupposes solidity. Hence we cannot think of them as solid either. Thus, Hume argues, if an object lacks secondary qualities, as the modern philosophy correctly teaches is true of *all* objects except perceptions, it lacks primary qualities also. And hence 'upon the whole [we] must conclude, that after the exclusion of colours, sounds, heat and cold, from the rank of external existences, there remains nothing, which can afford us a just and consistent idea of body' (Hume 1978: 229).

This argument exhibits Hume in his most sceptical mood, and indeed, it is at this point that Hume abandons the distinction he has insisted on hitherto between the principles of reason and the principles of the mere imagination. For it turns out that there are irrefutable arguments, based on principles which are 'permanent, irresistable and universal' (Hume 1978: 224) and which belong to what he has previously referred to as 'reason', for the conclusion that matter does not exist; on the other hand, it is impossible to believe this conclusion, for the mechanisms of the imagination which generate the belief in an external world are equally irresistible. Thus our common belief in an external world is indubitable, but in no way justified and, being false, incapable of any justification.

Chapter Five

The self and personal identity

The fiction of personal identity

Hume discusses personal identity in two places: in the main body of the *Treatise*, in section VI of Part IV of Book I, entitled 'Of personal identity', and in an Appendix published a year later with Book III. In the latter he declares himself wholly dissatisfied with his treatment of the topic in the main body of the *Treatise*, but confesses that he now finds the whole matter a 'labyrinth' and that he knows neither how to correct his former opinions nor how to render them consistent: there is no discussion of the topic in the *Enquiry Concerning Human Understanding* (Hume 1975).

Unfortunately Hume fails to make clear in his recantation what he finds objectionable in his earlier account, and though commentators have produced a variety of suggestions, no consensus as to what Hume's worry was has emerged. We shall return briefly to this matter later. First we need to be clear about what the problem is that Hume is concerned with in the section 'Of personal identity', and what solution he there offers to that problem.

In the tradition in which Hume was writing, deriving from Locke, the problem of personal identity was seen as that of giving an account of what constitutes personal identity. Locke's own answer to this question has two components, a negative component and a positive component. The negative component is that personal identity is not constituted by identity of substance, whether material or immaterial, any more than is identity of man: 'it being one thing to be the same substance, another the same man, and a third the same person' (*Essay* II, xxvii.7). The positive component is that what does constitute personal identity is sameness of consciousness: 'And as far as this consciousness can be extended backwards to any past action or thought, so far reaches the identity of that person' (*Essay* II, xxvii.9).

Thus, Locke asserts, combining the two components, 'it being the same consciousness that makes a man be himself to himself, personal identity depends on that only, whether it be annexed only to one individual substance or can be continued in a succession of several' (*Essay* II, xxvii.9).

In subsequent discussions reacting to Locke the role of substance in the constitution of personal identity became the key issue, and Butler, Reid and Leibniz all restored, in their accounts, the link that Locke had broken between personal identity and substantial identity (see Butler 1736; Reid 1941; Leibniz 1981).

If we read Hume as contributing to this debate on the constitution of personal identity we must understand his main contention to be an emphatic endorsement of the negative component of Locke's account: personal identity is not constituted by identity of substance. But, in fact, to read Hume in this way is to misunderstand him. For, according to Hume, personal identity is a fiction; the ascription of identity over time to persons, a mistake. It is an explicable mistake, and one we all necessarily make, but nonetheless, a mistake. For persons just do not endure self-identically over time. For Hume, the only problem that exists is thus the genetic one of specifying the psychological causes of the universal but mistaken belief in the existence of enduring persons, and this is the problem to which he addresses himself in his discussion of personal identity.

However, it is not, of course, in Hume's view, a peculiarity of persons that they do not endure self-identically over time; nor does anything else that we ordinarily think of as doing so. For, as we know, Hume thinks that the idea of identity is incompatible with the idea of change: it is the idea of an object which 'remains invariable and uninterrupted thro' a suppos'd variation of time' (Hume 1978: 253). Most, if not all objects of ordinary discourse, plants, animals, artefacts and the rest, are like persons in failing to satisfy this definition, and so when we ascribe identity to them, Hume says, it is only in an 'improper sense'. Thus, for Hume, the genetic problem of accounting for our false belief in the existence of enduring persons is just a part of the wider genetic problem of accounting for our false belief in the identity over time of changing things in general. In fact, he thinks, the same mechanism of the imagination which accounts for our ascriptions of identity over time to plants, animals and so on can equally well account for our ascriptions of identity over time to persons. This is because 'The identity which we ascribe to the mind of man, is only a fictitious one and *of a like kind* with that which we ascribe to vegetable and animal bodies. It cannot, therefore, have a different origin, but must proceed from a like operation of the imagination' (Hume 1978: 253, my italics).

The mechanism that generates the belief in the fiction of personal identity (the identity we ascribe to 'the mind of man') is the operation by which the mind is led to ascribe an identity to distinct perceptions, however interrupted or variable, which Hume has earlier appealed to in his account of the genesis of our belief in an external world.

He summarizes its manner of action as follows:

> In order to justify to ourselves this absurdity [i.e. the ascription of identity to distinct perceptions], we often feign some new and unintelligible principle, that connects the objects together, and prevents their interruption or variation. Thus we feign the continued existence of the perceptions of our senses to remove the interruption; and run into the notion of a soul, and self and substance, to disguise the variation, we may farther observe, that where we do not give rise to such a fiction, our propensity to confound identity with relation is so great, that we are apt to imagine something unknown and mysterious, connecting the parts, beside

their relation; and this I take to be the case with regard to the identity we ascribe to plants and vegetables. And even when this does not take place, we will feel a propensity to confound these ideas, tho' we are not fully able to satisfy ourselves in that particular, nor find anything invariable and uninterrupted to justify our notion of identity.

(Hume 1978: 254–5)

The important point to note is that it is an essential element of this story that the propensity we have to identify distinct perceptions is a propensity to regard them as answering to the idea of identity which Hume himself defines: 'an object that remains invariable and uninterrupted thro' a supposed variation of time'. If this were not our idea of identity then the psychological mechanism could not operate as he suggests. If, for instance, our idea of identity were consistent with the idea of interruption (that is, if we thought it possible that one object could have two beginnings of existence) then our propensity to identify (resembling but) temporally separated perceptions would not lead us to 'feign the continued existence of the perceptions of our senses' to remove the interruption, and thus would not lead us to our belief in an external world. Equally, if we thought of identity over time as consistent with change we would not be disposed to 'run into the notion of a soul, and self and substance' or be 'apt to imagine something unknown and mysterious' to disguise the variations. Thus, it is essential to Hume's account that our idea of identity is, in fact, the one he describes, and it is because this is so that he says:

[T]he controversy concerning identity is not merely a dispute of words. For when we attribute identity ... to variable or interrupted objects, our mistake is not confined to the expression, but is commonly attended with a fiction, either of something invariable and uninterrupted, or of something mysterious and inexplicable, or at least with a propensity to such fictions.

(Hume 1978: 225)

Thus, according to Hume, given that our idea of identity is as he describes, we must be in error in ascribing identity over time to 'variable or interrupted' things – ourselves included. But given that this is in fact our idea of identity, plus the rest of the genetic story he tells, this error is an explicable one.

The reification of perceptions

Although Hume's insistence that our notion of identity is the one he analyses provides him with a sufficient ground for his contention that personal identity is a fiction, it is not his only ground. Another is his conception of what the nature of the self or mental subject would have to be, if it existed and, correlatively, his view of the status of perceptions.

One of the best known passages in Hume's discussion of personal identity – indeed, one of the most famous passages in any philosophical text – is his denial that he is introspectively aware of any self or mental substance:

> For my part, when I enter most intimately into what I call myself, I always stumble on some particular perception or other, of heat or cold, light or shade, love or hatred, pain or pleasure. I never can catch myself at any time without a perception, and never can observe anything but the perception.

(Hume 1978: 252)

Many philosophers who have read this denial have found themselves in agreement. But the passage is a puzzling one. Hume writes as if it is just a matter of fact that on looking into himself he fails to find anything but perceptions, but this sits ill with his emphatic denial that he has any idea of a self distinct from perceptions. I can be confident that I am not observing a tea-kettle now because I know what it would be like to be doing so. But if Hume has no idea of a self he presumably has no conception of what it would be like to observe one. In that case, however, how does he know that he is not doing so? Maybe he is, but just fails to recognize the fact.

Another difficulty is that, as Chisholm puts it (1976: 39), it looks very much as though the self that Hume professes to be unable to find is the one that he finds to be stumbling – stumbling onto different perceptions. For Hume reports the results of his introspection in the first person: 'I never catch myself without a perception', 'I never observe anything but the perception'. Nor can he avoid doing so, if the basis of his denial is merely empirical. For suppose instead of 'I never observe anything but perceptions' he had written 'Nothing but perceptions is ever observed'. Then his assertion would have committed him to denying that anyone ever observes anything but perceptions, and so would have gone far beyond the evidence available to him. For how could he know that? As he himself writes a little later:

> If anyone upon serious and unprejudic'd reflection, thinks he has a different notion of himself, I must confess I can reason no longer with him. All I can allow him is, that he may be in the right as well as I, and that we are essentially different in that particular. He may, perhaps, perceive something simple and continu'd which he calls himself, tho' I am certain [that] there is no such principle in me.
>
> (Hume 1978: 252)

Of course, this is irony, for Hume immediately goes on: 'But setting aside some metaphysicians of this kind, I may venture to affirm of the rest of mankind, that they are nothing but a bundle or collection of different perceptions' (Hume 1978: 252). But Hume is not entitled to the irony, or to any claim about the rest of mankind if, as he represents it, the basis of his report of his negative finding is empirical. For to be so entitled he needs to be able to assent not merely to the (apparently self-defeating) claim that he never finds anything but perceptions, but also to the subjectless claim that nothing but perceptions is ever found.

Hume's denial is not therefore the straightforward empirical assertion it might at first appear to be. What then is his basis for it?

Once again, we must recall that Hume reifies perceptions. Thus he starts from a conception of mental states according to which for a person to be in a mental state is for a certain relational statement to be true of that person: that he is perceiving a certain sort of perception. But if this is correct it is very natural that Hume should deny the introspective observability of the self. For if to be in any mental state is to possess a relational property, then no mental state can be an intrinsic quality of its subject. Given that the only states of which one can be introspectively aware are mental, then, introspective awareness of a self would require awareness of it without any awareness of its intrinsic qualities. But surely it makes no sense to speak of observing something introspectively if the thing has no intrinsic qualities whatsoever which one can observe by introspection. As Shoemaker (1986) puts it, this makes no more sense than it does to speak of seeing or feeling a point in empty space.

The introspective inaccessibility of the self is thus an obvious consequence of the conception of all mental states as relational which follows from Hume's reification of perceptions. And the same line of thought can be pressed further. For Hume was undoubtedly enough of a dualist to take it for granted that a mental subject would have no intrinsic qualities that were not mental. But, if so, it follows from the Humean conception of the mental that a self can have no intrinsic qualities at all – it must be a 'bare particular' whose only properties are relational. However, it is not hard to see how someone thinking this could conclude that no such thing could exist.

These simple reflections suffice, I think, to explain Hume's confidence in his denial of the introspective accessibility of the self. But they can be taken further if we now turn from what the Humean conception of the mental implies about the subject of mental states – namely, that its only properties are relational ones – to what it implies about their objects, Hume's perceptions. What the conception implies, of course, is that these perceptions are things, indeed substances, and logically capable of existing independently of being perceived. And, as we have seen, Hume is emphatic that this is the case. Indeed, Hume thinks that everything which can be conceived is a substance (Hume 1978: 233), since nothing is logically dependent for its existence on anything else. Everything we conceive might have been the only thing in the whole universe. This, as we have seen, is a consequence Hume explicitly draws from the conjunction of the Separability Principle and the Conceivability Principle (Hume 1978: 233).

To make this consequence more vivid John Cook (1968) suggests that it follows from Hume's position that there could be a scratch or a dent without there being anything scratched or dented and, indeed, that the Cheshire cat's separated grin is a logical possibility.

Cook suggests that the flaw in Hume's reasoning that this brings out can be expressed as follows: the fact that x is distinct from y does not entail that it is distinguishable from y, not, at least, if this is to entail that 'x exists' is to be compatible with 'y does not exist'. For the fact that x is distinct from y does not entail that x can be identified independently of y. Thus, the dent in my fender is distinct from my fender: 'the dent in my fender' does not stand for the same object as 'my fender'. But the dent is not distinguishable from the fender – I could not get someone to understand which dent I was referring to without identifying the fender in which it was a dent. Hence, Cook thinks, we can deny that Hume's argument establishes that dents are substances and by parity of reasoning we can deny that it establishes that perceptions are substances.

However, Hume has a response available. For he can insist that distinctness does entail independence, and, by appealing to his account of 'distinctions of reason', outlined in chapter 2, can deny that he is committed to the absurdity that the dent might exist in the absence of the fender. For, he can say, the dent is in fact the very same object as the fender, and its distinctness is merely a distinction of reason. In fact, it is precisely to deal with such apparent counter-examples to his denial of real connections between distinct existences that Hume develops his account of distinctions of reason.

To this it can be rejoined, however, that if the appeal to the idea that the distinction in question is merely a distinction of reason can be allowed in this case, there is no reason not to apply it also to the distinction between the self and its perceptions, and so Hume's argument does not, after all, establish the substantiality of perceptions. Or, to put the point differently, we can allow that it follows from the conjunction of the Separability Principle and the Conceivability Principle that 'whatever can be conceived' is a substance, but then it simply becomes debatable what can be conceived. Not dents, if they are to be disallowed as substances; but if not, why must perceptions be admitted as conceivable?

It appears, then, that at bottom Hume's argument for the substantiality of perceptions may be question begging. But the important point for our purposes is not what Hume's argument does prove, but what he thinks it proves. For if perceptions are thought of as substances, i.e. as logically ontologically independent entities, then the self, thought of as that which has perceptions, must now appear to have a very problematic status indeed. It is implicit in this conception of the self, whether or not it is thought of as introspectively observable, that it is thought of as having a special ontological status vis-à-vis its perceptions and not merely as being ontologically on a par with them. And, of course, this is quite right. But it is quite right just because being in a mental state is not to be understood as bearing a special relation of 'perception' to something which has a (logically) independent existence, any more than smiling or walking is to be understood as bearing a certain special relation (of 'wearing' or 'taking') to an entity (a smile or a walk) logically capable of an independent existence. The grammar of the noun 'perception' (and that of 'idea' and 'impression') is like that of 'smile' or 'walk'. The concept of someone's having a perception is logically prior to the concept of a perception.

But Hume, in claiming that perceptions are logically ontologically independent, denies this, and thus denies the only possible basis for regarding the self, qua perceiver, as ontologically prior to its perceptions. That he should claim that the self is in reality nothing but a bundle of its perceptions in the section following is thus entirely intelligible. Once perceptions are reified as substances no other conception of the self makes any sense at all.

Once again, Cook's (1968) remarks are perceptive. He points out that if the argument Hume gives were a good one then it would establish that not only perceptions but qualities generally are logically capable of an independent existence, and indeed Hume applies the argument to yield this conclusion himself (1978: 222). If so, Descartes' (1984) famous analogy in the *Second Meditation*, in which he compares the relation between a piece of wax and its qualities to the relation between a man and his clothes, would be an appropriate one. But one consequence of this analogy is that the wax is represented as hidden beneath its garments and so as in itself unobservable. This is because the analogy implies that the assertion that the wax has any quality is in reality an assertion of a relation between it and something else. And a second consequence of the analogy is that the qualities of the wax are represented as being themselves substantial, as though they can 'stand by themselves', as a suit of armour can when no man is wearing it. But these consequences of the analogy, which is an appropriate one if the Humean argument is a good one, make it obvious that if the wax is so conceived, its existence, as anything other than that of a collection of qualities, must be regarded as highly problematic. Exactly the same is true of the self if Hume's argument is correct.

The rejection of the substantial self

With this background in mind we can now turn to the details of Hume's section on personal identity. In fact this section is continuous with the preceding one, which though entitled 'Of the immateriality of the soul', contains a critique of both materialist and immaterialist doctrines of a substantial self, together with the striking criticism of the 'doctrine of the immateriality, simplicity and indivisibility of a thinking substance' that 'it is a true atheism, and will serve to justify all those sentiments, for which Spinoza is so universally infamous' (Hume 1978: 240). The basis of this last criticism is again Hume's conception of perceptions as ontologically independent entities:

There are two different systems of beings presented, to which I suppose myself under a necessity of assigning some ... ground of inhesion. I observe first the universe of objects or of body: the sun, moon, stars ... Here Spinoza ... tells me that these are only modifications; and that the subject, in which they inhere is simple, incompounded, and indivisible. After this I consider the other system of beings, viz. the universe of thought, or my impressions and ideas. There I observe *another* sun, moon and stars. ... Upon my enquiring ... Theologians ... tell me, that these also are modifications ... of one simple substance. Immediately ... I am deafn'd with ... a hundred voices, that treat the first hypothesis with

detestation and scorn ... and the second with applause and venera-
tion ... I turn my attention to these hypotheses ... and find that
they have the same fault of being unintelligible ... and that ... any
absurdity in one ... is ... common to both.

(Hume 1978: 234, my italics)

Nor are matters improved for the Theologians, according to
Hume:

[I]f instead of calling thought a modification of the soul, we ... give
it the more ... modish name of an action. By an action we mean ...
something which, properly speaking, is neither distinguishable,
nor separable from its substance ... But nothing is gained by this
change. ... First ... the word action, according to this explication of
it, can never be justly apply'd to any perception. ... [In] the second
place ... may not the Atheists likewise take possession of [the word
action], and affirm that plants, animals, men, etc., are nothing but
particular actions of one simple ... substance? ... 'tis impossible to
discover any absurdity in [this] supposition ... which will not be
applicable to a like supposition concerning impressions and ideas.

(Hume 1978: 245–6)

There could not, I think, be a clearer illustration than this of the
lengths to which Hume is prepared to go in following through the
consequences of his reification of perceptions – if a tree cannot be
a modification of Spinoza's God, my idea of a tree cannot be a
modification of me!

Turning now to the section 'Of personal identity' Hume proceeds very rapidly, and confidently, for reasons that I hope will
now be perfectly understandable, to his conclusion that the self is
nothing more than a bundle of perceptions. The whole business
takes less than two pages.

Some philosophers have thought that 'we are every moment
intimately conscious of what we call our SELF.' But: 'Unluckily all
these positive assertions are contrary to that very experience
which is pleaded for them, nor have we any idea of self, after the
manner it is here explained, for from what impression could this
idea be derived?' Since the self is supposed to be an unchanging
object any impression of self must be constantly the same

throughout the whole course of our lives. But, Hume finds, looking within himself, 'There is no impression constant and invariable. Pain and pleasure, grief and joy ... succeed each other. ... It cannot therefore, be from any of these impressions, or from any other that the idea of self is deriv'd; and consequently there is no such idea' (Hume 1978: 251–2).

Hume goes on to raise explicitly the difficulty that his conception of perceptions as ontologically independent creates for the notion of a substantial self:

> But farther, what must become of all our particular perceptions upon this hypothesis? All these are different, and distinguishable, and separable from each other, and may be separately consider'd, and may exist separately, and have no need of any thing to support their existence. After what manner therefore do they belong to self; and how are they connected with it?

> (Hume 1978: 252)

It is immediately after this that he issues his denial of the observability of a self distinct from perceptions, and concludes that the self can be nothing but a bundle of perceptions.

So much, then, for Hume's arguments for the bundle theory of the self. Taken together with his analysis of identity, they entitle him, he believes, to the conclusion that personal identity is a fiction, that 'the mind is a kind of theatre, where several perceptions successively make their appearance. ... There is properly no simplicity in it at one time, nor identity in different' (Hume 1978: 253). For the idea of identity is that of an object, that 'remains invariable and uninterrupted thro' a suppos'd variation of time'. But if the bundle theory is correct a person is nothing but a sequence of different (ontologically independent) objects existing in succession, and connected by a close relation – something like a thunderstorm. But 'as such a succession answers perfectly to our notion of diversity, it can only be by [a] mistake that we ascribe to it an identity' (Hume 1978: 255).

The only question that remains then, Hume thinks, is to explain the psychological mechanism that accounts for this mistake.

Hume's account of the source of the mistake

Hume summarizes his account of this as follows. In contemplating an identical, i.e., an invariable and unchanging object, we are doing something very different from contemplating a succession of objects related by links of resemblance, causation and contiguity, but:

> That action of the imagination, by which we consider the uninterrupted and invariable object, and that by which we reflect on the succession of related objects, are almost the same to the feeling. ... The relation facilitates the transmission of the mind from one object to another, and renders its passage as smooth as if it contemplated one continu'd object. This resemblance is the cause of the confusion and mistake, and makes us substitute the notion of identity, instead of that of related objects. However at one instant we may consider the related succession as variable or interrupted, we are sure the next to ascribe to it a perfect identity, and regard it as invariable and uninterrupted.
>
> (Hume 1978: 254)

Hume's discussion of personal identity is merely the last of several discussions in which he appeals to this mechanism. The first, in the section 'Of scepticism with regard to the senses', we have already encountered.

The next operation of the mechanism Hume explains is that which produces our, or rather the 'antient philosophers', belief in substance:

> 'Tis evident, that as the ideas of the several distinct successive qualities of objects are united together by a very close relation, the mind, in looking along the succession, must be carry'd from one part of it to another by an easy transition. ... The smooth and uninterrupted progress of the thought ... readily deceives the mind, and makes us ascribe an identity to the changeable succession of connected qualities. But when we ... survey at once any two distinct periods of its duration ... the variations ... do now appear of consequence, and seem entirely to destroy the identity. ... In order to reconcile which contradictions the imagination is apt to feign

> something unknown and invisible, which it supposes to continue
> the same under all variations; and this unintelligible something it
> calls ... substance or original and first matter.

(Hume 1978: 220)

Once again the story is one of conflation and error produced by
the faculty of 'fancy' or 'imagination'.

It is exactly the same, Hume thinks, in the case of personal
identity. The same mechanism of the imagination is at work and it
produces conflation and error in just the same way. The succession
of my perceptions is merely a succession of distinct related objects.
But because the objects in the succession are closely related the
action of the imagination in surveying the succession is 'almost
the same to the feeling' as the action of the imagination in considering an uninterrupted and invariable object. As in the other
cases, the similarity between the two acts of mind leads me to confound the two situations and thus to regard the succession of
related perceptions as really united by identity. And so I am led to
believe in the unity of the self, which is as much a fiction as in the
other cases of the operation of the mechanism, and, 'proceed[s]
entirely from the smooth and uninterrupted progress of the
thought along a train of connected ideas according to the principles
above explain'd' (Hume 1978: 260). Notice, however, this difference. In the case of the operation of the mechanism to produce the
belief in the self, as in the case of its operation to produce the
belief in substance or original and first matter, Hume does not
distinguish 'vulgar' and 'philosophical' variants of the belief to be
explained, as he does in the case of belief in the external world.
This is because his attention in the last case is on the conflict
between identity and interruptedness, whereas in the former two
cases it is on the conflict between identity and variation. Thus in
the last case, space is left for the vulgar view because it is not self-
evidently absurd to deny interruptedness, given resemblance, so,
unlike variation, it can be 'removed' and not merely 'disguised'
(Hume 1978: 254–5). On Hume's account, then, our everyday
belief in an enduring self is on a par with the ancient philosophers'
fiction of substance and first matter, which he has characterised in

section VI as arising from principles which are neither universal nor unavoidable in human nature, or else on a par with the modern philosopher's theory of double existence, which he has characterized as a monstrous offspring of two principles, with no primary recommendation to the imagination. Possibly, though there is no evidence that this is so, his belated recognition of this explains his Appendix recantation.

All that remains to be explained, Hume thinks, is what relations do link my successive perceptions so as to bring about this uninterrupted progress of the thought. His answer is resemblance and causation.

Our perceptions at successive times resemble each other for a variety of reasons, of course, but the one Hume stresses is that people can remember their past experience:

> For what is the memory, but a faculty by which we raise up the images of past perceptions? And as an image necessarily resembles its object must not the frequent placing of these resembling perceptions in the chain of thought, convey the imagination more easily from one link to another, and make the whole like the continuance of one object?
>
> (Hume 1978: 260–1)

Given this copy theory of memory Hume is able to regard memory not merely as providing us with access to our past selves, but also as contributing to the bundles of perceptions which we can survey, elements which represent, and thus resemble, earlier elements; and so – since resemblance is a relation which enables the mind to slide smoothly along a succession of perceptions – as strengthening our propensity to believe in the fiction of a continuing self. In this particular case, then, Hume is able to say, with a nod of agreement to Locke, 'memory not only discovers the identity but contributes to its production' (Hume 1978: 261).

But we do not remember all, or even most of, our past actions or experiences. Yet we do not affirm, because we have entirely forgotten the incidents of certain past days, that the present self is not the same person as the self of that time. Consequently there must be something else which enables us to think of our identity as extending beyond our memory.

Here Hume appeals to causality, which has been previously introduced in his account of:

> [T]he true idea of the human mind ... a system of different perceptions or different existences, which are linked together by the relation of cause and effect. ... In this respect I cannot compare the soul more properly to anything than to a republic or commonwealth, in which the several members are united by the reciprocal ties of government and subordination, and give rise to other persons, who propagate the same republic in the incessant changes of its parts.
>
> (Hume 1978: 266)

When we think of ourselves as existing at times we cannot remember we do so, Hume says, by imagining the chain of causes and effects that we remember extending beyond our memory of them. So the causal links between our perceptions, as well as their resemblances, are crucial to our belief in a continuing self which exists at times it no longer recalls. Consequently, Hume is able to say, this time in agreement with Locke's opponents: 'In this view ... memory does not so much produce as discover personal identity, by shewing us the relation of cause and effect among our different perceptions' (Hume 1978: 262).

Objections to Hume

Two objections must be noted at the outset. First, Hume is just wrong to reify perceptions or to think of them as capable of an independent existence. The comparison of the mind to a republic and of its perceptions to the citizens of the republic is thus fundamentally flawed. Second, Hume is again just wrong to think that identity must be incompatible with change. Whether this is so depends on the kind of thing to which identity is being ascribed. Some things may be by definition unchanging things, but in the case of most things this is not so. They cannot survive just any change, but what kind of changes they can survive depends on the kind of thing they are. To know what such changes are is part of knowing the definition of the kind. And persons, in particular, are entities that can survive many changes without ceasing to exist (Penelhum 1955 is the classic source of this second criticism.)

These are radical objections. If correct they show that the whole Humean enterprise is misconceived from the start. I think that they do show this. But there are other objections even if these are set aside.

One of the most obvious is the following. We not only regard ourselves as unified selves, we also have particular beliefs about which perceptions are ours. But it is not the case that all the perceptions we ascribe to ourselves are related either by resemblance or by causality. In particular, this is not true of what Hume calls 'impressions of sensation'. At present I have an impression of a desktop partly covered with sheets of writing paper. If I turn my head to the left I have an impression of a bookcase filled with books. The impression of the desktop neither resembles nor is a cause of the impression of the bookcase (nor is the desk top itself a cause of the bookcase); yet I regard both impressions as mine. Why, on Hume's story, should this be so? According to the story we are led to ascribe perceptions to a single self only when we have a propensity to identify them; and such a propensity is produced only if the action of the mind in surveying them resembles that in surveying a constant and uninterrupted object. But in the present case this will not be so. On Hume's account, therefore, I ought to have no inclination to regard both these perceptions as mine. But I do.

This criticism of Hume can be deepened by recalling his views on causality. According to these causality is not a relation we perceive between objects; rather we regard a pair of objects as related as cause and effect when we have observed a constant conjunction of similar pairs of contiguous objects and, as a consequence of this observed constant conjunction, are led to expect the second member of the pair on perceiving the first. For two of my perceptions to be related as cause and effect, then, is for them to be an instance of an observed constant conjunction between similar pairs of perceptions that has produced in me a disposition to expect the second member of such a pair whenever I perceive the first. And this is to say that for my perceptions to be causally linked in the way Hume suggests (Hume 1978: 261) they would have to exhibit a multitude of long-standing constant conjunctions. But they do not do so.

Once one puts Hume's views on causality together with his account of the genesis of our belief in personal identity, therefore, it becomes evident that the latter requires the possession by the human mind of a good deal more regularity and less novelty than it actually has.

The converse objection to the one just stated is worth considering. Not only do perceptions which we self-ascribe fail to be related by resemblance or causality in the way Hume requires; these relations do obtain between perceptions which we do not self-ascribe. Many of one's perceptions are bound to resemble those of others, given that we all inhabit the same world. Presumably, also, one's perceptions, one's mental states, sometimes stand in causal connections with those of others, for instance when one talks with them. Why, then, am I not disposed to regard (some of) your perceptions as mine? Why, on the contrary, do I think of you and I as having separate minds?

Of course, Hume has an easy answer to this question. Your perceptions are not available to me as input to the mechanism which generates my belief in the unity of my mind; for I cannot 'look into your breast', as Hume puts it, and observe them. Hence the fact that they stand in relations of resemblance and causality to my perceptions and thus would be self-ascribed by me if I could observe them is neither here nor there.

But this defence of Hume merely gets us to the crux of the matter. The Humean story requires that perceptions be pre-bundled, as it were, before the belief-producing mechanism he describes can operate. So Hume cannot after all reject the meta-physical–ontological question of what in fact distinguishes one mind from another and what in fact unifies the elements within a single mind. For the genetic–psychological question that he explicitly addresses presupposes that this other question is answerable.

This is not to say that the metaphysical–ontological question is not answerable in Humean terms. Obviously any simple appeal to relations of resemblance and causality is bound to fail, given what we have already seen. But maybe some ingenious construction out of these relations might individuate minds in a way that fits our pre-philosophical ideas. However, Hume never addresses this question and says nothing that makes it seem at all likely that this might be so. We shall see in a moment that there is, given Hume's assumptions, strong reason for supposing that it could not be so.

The same point – that the Humean story requires that minds be 'pre-bundled' antecedently to the operation of the belief-producing mechanism Hume describes – emerges again if we look at another obvious criticism of Hume's account.

This is the criticism that Hume's account of how we mistakenly come to believe in the existence of a unitary self itself presupposes the existence of unitary selves. For the story Hume tells can be true only if the mind (or the 'imagination'), as a result of surveying a certain succession of perceptions, is mistakenly led to believe in the existence of a unitary self. But if that belief is mistaken what is it that surveys the sequence of perceptions and is led into this error? Does it not seem that it must be a unitary entity of precisely the type Hume repudiates?

In short, on the face of it, the explanatory story Hume tells seems internally inconsistent. What he says is that the mind, as a result of surveying a certain sort of sequence of perceptions, is caused to have a mistaken belief in the existence of a unitary self. But since 'mind' and 'self' are in this context interchangeable this seems to mean, quite absurdly: the mind, as a result of surveying a certain sequence of perceptions, is caused to have a mistaken belief in its own existence.

And, a proponent of this criticism might add, perhaps Hume himself half-recognizes the difficulty he faces. For it is a notable fact about the section on personal identity that, despite the fact that the primary object of Hume's account must be to explain the belief each of us has in his own identity, the perspective from which he presents the problem is determinedly third-personal. In fact, this comes out even in his manner of posing the central question of the section 'whether in pronouncing concerning the identity of a person we observe some real bond among his perceptions, or only feel one among the ideas we form of them' (Hume 1978: 259).

This is the most obvious objection to Hume's discussion of personal identity. But, as Pike (1967) demonstrates, it is far from clear that it is a good one. According to Hume each mind is nothing but a bundle of perceptions. And so for a mind to perform a mental act is simply for a perception to occur in it. The mind's 'activity' consists in nothing more than perceptions occurring in it. Of course, it seems odd to say 'a bundle of perceptions confuses certain sequences of perceptions with others' (say), but that is merely because it is out of line with our ordinary manner of speaking. But that manner of speaking, according to Hume, embodies a falsehood.

What goes for the mind's activities also goes for its propensities or dispositions. They must be regarded as dispositions of certain bundles of perceptions to develop in certain ways over time. For example, the cash value of the claim that we are all disposed to confuse constant but interrupted series of perceptions with similar uninterrupted series is just that whenever an uninterrupted series of perceptions occurs in the particular bundle which is someone's mind, and then a similar but interrupted series occurs there, that mind or bundle will also come to contain the lively idea, or belief, that the second series is like the first.

Thus, it seems, Hume's enterprise is not self-defeating in the way in which the objection under discussion envisages. For he can reinterpret talk of the mind's activities or dispositions in a way that is consistent with his belief that all that really exist are bundles of ontologically independent perceptions.

But, of course, not all bundles of perceptions will display the patterns of development that correspond, in Hume's view, to the dispositions and propensities he ascribes to minds. These patterns of development will be displayed only by certain bundles of perceptions – what we might call 'personal' bundles. But now, which are they?

We have come back to the point that Hume needs an answer not only to the genetic–psychological question: 'What causes induce us to believe in unitary selves?', but also to the metaphysical–ontological question: 'What in fact unites the perceptions within a single mind and distinguishes one mind from another?' For the picture with which he operates, and with which he cannot dispense, is of perceptions objectively tied together in well-individuated bundles, prior to the operation of the belief-forming mechanism which generates, in each bundle which qualifies as a mind, a belief in its own unity.

As I said previously, Hume tells us nothing that suggests that he might be able to provide a good answer to this question. But matters are worse than that. For as Don Garrett has argued (1981), given Hume's views about causation, the relations of causation and resemblance, or any however ingenious construction there-from, are necessarily insufficient to provide an answer to the metaphysical–ontological question, necessarily insufficient to provide an 'idea of the human mind' that corresponds to our actual idea, even after that has been purged of its vague association with metaphysical substance.

Garrett argues the point thus: when we regard a pair of objects as related as cause and effect, according to Hume, all that is object-ively present in the situation is precedence and contiguity in time or place. In addition there will have been an observed constant conjunction of similar pairs of objects in like relations of prece-dency and contiguity, as a result of which we are led, mistakenly, to regard the objects as necessarily connected.

Two exactly resembling perceptions in distinct minds can differ in their causal relations, therefore, only by differing in their relations of precedence or contiguity to other perceptions. But simultaneous exactly resembling perceptions occurring in dis-tinct minds can differ in their causal relations only by differing in their spatial locations. However, Hume is emphatic that many, in fact most, of our perceptions do not have spatial locations. This indeed is one of his main theses in the section immediately pre-ceding his discussion of personal identity, and one of the principal components of his argument against a materialist conception of the self. He asserts:

[A]n object may exist and yet be nowhere, and I assert ... this is not only possible, but that the greatest part of beings do and must exist after this manner. ... This is evidently the case with all our

135

perceptions ... except those of the sight and feeling. A moral reflection cannot be plac'd on the right or on the left hand of a passion, nor can a smell or sound be either of a circular or a square figure. These objects and perceptions, so far from requiring any particular place, are absolutely incompatible with it, and even the imagination cannot attribute it to them.

(Hume 1978: 235–6)

But, of course, if there are two exactly resembling and simultaneous perceptions, x and y, in distinct minds, neither of which is spatially located – two moral reflections or two passions, say – they cannot fail to stand to all other perceptions in exactly the same relations of resemblance and causality. If there is a bundle of perceptions containing x which qualifies as a mind in virtue of all its members' being interrelated by some relation constructed out of resemblance and causality, there will be an exactly similar bundle of perceptions consisting of all the rest of the perceptions in the first bundle together with y instead of x. And the Humean account will be quite incapable of saying why this bundle also should not qualify as a mind.

However complicated an account, in terms of resemblance and causality, Hume might give in attempting to answer the metaphysical – ontological question concerning the principle of individuation for minds, then, it must necessarily be inadequate. For any two qualitatively identical perceptions that are neither of sight nor touch and occur simultaneously will be incapable of being distinguished either by their similarity relations or by their causal relations. To be able to embrace such a 'Humean' principle of individuation for bundles one must, therefore, either abandon Hume's own most emphatically expressed view of the possibility of spatially unlocated perceptions, or reject the common-sense view that qualitatively identical perceptions may occur in two minds at the same time; in which case one can hardly claim to be giving an account of the unity of the mind in any sense that at all approximates to the one we actually have.

In presenting these criticisms of Hume's theory I have not suggested that they were the source of his subsequent dissatisfaction with his account. Whether they were, or whether it was some quite different difficulty that was worrying Hume, it is quite impossible to say. Hume is far too inexplicit. All he says is:

> [A]ll my hopes vanish, when I come to explain the principles, that unite our successive perceptions in our thought or consciousness. I cannot discover any theory, which gives me satisfaction on this head. ... In short, there are two principles, which I cannot render consistent; nor is it in my power to renounce either of them, viz. that all our distinct perceptions are distinct existences, and that the mind never perceives any real connexion among distinct existences.
>
> (Hume 1978: 635–6)

Clearly Hume no longer believes that the belief-generating mechanism he has described is sufficient to generate the belief in a unitary self. But since, as all commentators have noted, the two principles he claims that he cannot render consistent clearly are consistent, he gives no clue as to why this is so.

chapter Six

Morality

Project and predecessors

Hume's main writings on morality are in Book III of the *Treatise*, the *Enquiry Concerning the Principles of Morals* and various supplementary essays, most notably 'Of the Standard of Taste'. Of these, he regarded the discussion in the *Enquiry* as his best. Nevertheless, Hume's most complete and complex discussion is in the *Treatise*, in which arguments occur which are not repeated in the *Enquiry*. In addition, an indispensable aid to understanding Hume's views on morality is his discussion of the passions in Book II of the *Treatise*, where he provides, in Part III, section III, 'Of the influencing motives of the Will', the foundation on which he builds, in Book III, his most famous argument about morality – that moral distinctions are not derived from reason.

Hume's moral philosophy is set against the background of ongoing disputes in the seventeenth and eighteenth centuries concerning the nature and foundations of morality and moral knowledge. His principal opponents were the rationalist moral philosophers, of whom Samuel Clarke was the most distinguished, and the 'moral sceptics' or 'egoists', particularly Thomas Hobbes, but also Bernard Mandeville. His greatest indebtedness was to

Francis Hutcheson, the chief proponent of the 'moral sense' theory of ethics. Thus Hume states at the outset of the moral *Enquiry* that his aim is to examine 'the controversy started of late concerning the general foundation of morals; whether they be derived from reason, or from sentiment' (Hume 1975: 170), and sides firmly with the sentimentalists. He also indicates his rejection of the views of the moral sceptics, those who 'deny the reality of moral distinctions' (Hume 1975: 169), whom he describes as 'disingenuous disputants', since it is not 'conceivable that any human creature could ever seriously believe that all characters and actions were alike entitled to the affection and regard of everyone'.

Let us now look briefly at the views of Clarke, Hobbes and Hutcheson in relation to those of Hume.

Samuel Clarke held that there are rational moral requirements on the wills of all intelligent beings. These arise from the 'necessary fitnesses or unfitnesses of certain manners of behaviour of some persons towards others', which obtain independently of God's will and determines our obligations towards others (Raphael 1991: 192). Our knowledge of these obligations, like our knowledge of mathematics, is a product of reason: 'Iniquity is the very same in action as falsity or contradiction in theory' (Raphael 1991: 207). Consequently: 'by this ... knowledge of ... the ... fitnesses of things, the wills ... of all intelligent beings are constantly directed, and must needs be determined to act accordingly; excepting those only who will things to be what they are not and cannot be' (Raphael 1991: 198–9).

Against this Hume holds that moral distinctions are not based on reason or argument, and they need not be the same to every intelligent being, but, like the perception of beauty and deformity, are 'founded entirely on the peculiar fabric and constitution of the human species' (Hume 1975: 170).

Hobbes was a materialist and moral relativist. In the world there is nothing but matter in motion. The secondary qualities – colour, sound and savour – belong to appearance, not to the objects themselves. Value is similarly not part of the real world. Hobbes calls 'delight' or 'pleasure', 'the appearance or sense of good' (Raphael 1991: 22). But he thinks that goodness is no more in the world than colour is. Parts of the world appear to our senses to be coloured, and parts appear to be good if we desire them, but in both cases this is mere appearance. Hence Hobbes' definition of good and evil: 'Whatsoever is the object of any man's appetite or desire; that is it that he for his part calleth good: and the object of his hate and aversion, evil. ... For these words of good, evil ... are ever used with relation to the person that useth them' (Raphael 1991: 21–2).

Hume himself makes Hobbes' comparison of values to colours and other secondary qualities. But he is emphatically opposed to Hobbes' relativism. In 'A Dialogue', published with the moral *Enquiry*, he writes:

> [T]he principles upon which men reason in morals are always the same; though the conclusions, which they draw, are often very different ... never was any quality recommended by anyone, as a virtue or moral excellence, but on account of its being useful or agreeable to a man himself, or to others.

(Hume 1975: 335–6)

The reasons why such qualities are morally approved of, Hume explains in the *Treatise*, is because of the human capacity for sympathy, by which we reflect the emotions and feelings of others: observing your pain causes me pain, and knowledge of your pleasure gives me pleasure. In the *Enquiry* Hume simply postulates a fundamental human capacity for general benevolence or 'humanity or fellow-feeling', to explain why no man can be absolutely indifferent to the happiness or misery of others, and seems to indicate that he now thinks the complicated *Treatise* explanation in terms of the associative mechanism of sympathy is, at least, unnecessary. But, whether in terms of sympathy or unanalysed benevolence, Hume remains confident that all human beings will respond similarly to the characteristics he lists as virtues and vices – at least, when they judge from a common point of view and set aside their private and particular situation (Hume 1975: 272), and, as he explains in the *Treatise*, it is 'only when a character is considered in general, without reference to our particular interest, that it causes such a feeling or sentiment, as denominates it morally good or evil' (Hume 1978: 472).

In his rejection of moral scepticism Hume follows Hutcheson, his immediate predecessor and the greatest influence on his moral theory, and perhaps on his philosophy in general. Hutcheson argues that the egoists cannot explain, amongst other things, why we respond differently to voluntary actions and natural events when both affect our interests equally, and how we respond to motives we perceive even when they do not issue in actions that affect us (Raphael 1991: 264–5). He also insists that it is just a fact that men do sometimes act out of a genuine sense of benevolence, and that this is a natural mode of behaviour.

Hutcheson defines moral goodness as 'the idea of some quality apprehended in actions which procures approbation'; moral evil is the idea of a contrary quality that arouses condemnation (Raphael 1991: 261). Approbation and condemnation are simple ideas that cannot be explained further, but we can observe them within ourselves in response to the actions and motives of those around us.

Thus a morally good motive for Hutcheson is simply that quality of an action whose apprehension causes us to approve of it. What this quality is, Hutcheson thinks, is a matter of empirically discoverable fact. It could turn out to be anything. In fact, it turns out to be the motive of benevolence. It is this motive, and this alone, which is the object of our moral sense.

Thus Hutcheson is a naturalist. His position is that virtue is that natural quality of human beings, i.e., benevolence, which in fact arouses the idea of approbation, and vice is that natural property which arouses the idea of disapprobation.

Hume's position differs from Hutcheson's in three ways. He is not satisfied, at least in the *Treatise*, simply to postulate simple ideas of approbation and disapprobation and describe moral sense merely as an 'original quality and primary constitution' (Hume 1978: 473) of the mind which disposes it to receive them. Instead he appeals to the associative mechanism of sympathy to explain the moral sense. Second, and relatedly, he does not think that we approve only of benevolence – there are other virtues, justice for one. And third, Hume is not a naturalist, or at least not unambiguously. For in the case of virtue, as in the case of causation, he thinks that in our moral judgements we 'spread our minds on the world'. 'Benevolence is an observable matter of fact in the world, but virtue or vice can never be found in the world till you turn your reflexion into your own breast, and find there a sentiment of approbation or disapprobation which arise in you towards the action' (Hume 1978: 469).

Let us now turn to details.

Reason and passion

Hume's rejection of the rationalist thesis that moral distinctions are derived from reason is based on his prior rejection, in Book II of the *Treatise*, of a widely held view of the role of reason in motivation, reported in the first paragraph of section III of Part III: 'Nothing is more usual in philosophy, and even in common life, than to talk of the combat of passion and reason, to give the preference to reason, and to assert that men are only so far virtuous as they conform themselves to its dictates' (Hume 1978: 413).

In opposition to this tradition Hume announces that he will prove 'first that reason alone can never be a motive to any action of the will; and secondly that it can never oppose passion in the direction of the will' (Hume 1978: 413), and concludes, famously, 'Reason is, and ought only to be the slave of the passions and can never pretend to any other office than to serve and obey them' (Hume 1978: 415).

To understand this we need to look first at Hume's theory of the passions, and then at what he means by 'reason'.

Our passions are our emotions, feelings and motives; they include love and hatred, pride and humility, desire and aversion, the sense of beauty and the sense of morality. What these all have in common is that they are impressions of reflection (or secondary impressions), which arise from other impressions (of sensation) or ideas. Significantly, the only impression of reflection Hume mentions before Book II is the impression of necessary connection.

Hume divides passions into the direct and the indirect, and independently into the calm and the violent.

The first distinction is explained as follows: 'By direct passions I understand such as arise immediately from good or evil, from pain or pleasure. By indirect such as proceed from the same principles, but by the complication of other qualities' (Hume 1978: 276).

Pride is Hume's paradigm indirect passion, desire and aversion his paradigm direct passions. Much later, in section IX of Part III of Book II of the *Treatise* (Hume 1978: 439), Hume notes the existence of direct passions that do not proceed from good and evil but 'arise from a natural impulse or instinct, which is perfectly unaccountable'. These include 'the desire of punishment to our enemies, and of happiness to our friends, hunger, lust and a few other bodily appetites'. Properly speaking, Hume says, these passions produce good and evil, rather than proceeding from them. He says little about them in the rest of the *Treatise*; it is not clear that if he had taken them seriously he would have needed to appeal to the mechanism of sympathy as extensively as he does, and in the moral *Enquiry*, where they are taken seriously (see below), sympathy is, as noted, no longer prominent.

The motivating passions Hume discusses are all direct; anticipating the discussion in Book III of the *Treatise* of the motivating power of moral sentiment, we can infer that feelings of moral approbation and disapprobation must count as direct passions.

The 'complication of other qualities' which distinguishes indirect passions becomes clearer when Hume give his analysis of the indirect passion of pride. He defines this as 'that agreeable impression, which arises in the mind, when the view either of our beauty, riches or power makes us satisfied with ourselves'. Pride is a simple impression but it is embedded in a complex causal structure involving both the idea of oneself and the idea of some object related to oneself, and it arises, as do all indirect passions, by a 'double association of impressions and ideas'. The story is as follows. Suppose I am proud of my beautiful house. Then the cause of my pride is my beautiful house. This cause is composed of a subject: my house, and a quality: its beauty (Hume 1978: 279). The idea of the subject, the house, because it is my house, brings about, by the association of ideas, the idea of myself. The idea of the quality causes an impression of pleasure, which, in turn, by the association of impressions (an associative mechanism Hume first introduces in Book II) brings about the resembling simple impression of pride (impressions, unlike ideas, are only associated by resemblance), which latter naturally directs the mind to the idea of the self. Thus the pleasure of pride is connected to the idea of self, the former being the effect of the idea of the cause via the association of impressions, the latter being the effect of the idea of the cause via the association of ideas.

Hume explains the other indirect passions, including humility, love and hatred by the same associative mechanism. Humility differs from pride solely in respect of the quality of the cause – something that causes displeasure rather than pleasure. Love differs from pride solely in respect of its object: another rather than oneself; and hatred relates to humility as love relates to pride.

The most important thing to note about this associative explanation is that vice and virtue are among the causes of pride and humility and love and hatred. Thus, the moral approbation and disapprobation to which these qualities give rise are the pleasurable and painful feelings that in turn cause, via the association of impressions, these indirect passions. My moral approval of myself causes my pride in myself; my moral disapprobation of myself causes my humility. My moral approval and disapproval of you causes the love or hatred I feel towards you.

It is while explaining the indirect passions that Hume introduces the mechanism of sympathy. He first introduces it to explain how the good opinion of others makes us proud (Hume 1978: 316). Briefly, the explanation is that via sympathy we are infected with the good opinions of others, as we may be infected by their diseases. In general, sympathy converts ideas into impressions, and hence the ideas of others' passions into the passions themselves. So, 'an angry or sorrowful [countenance] throws a sudden damp upon me' (Hume 1978: 317). I become aware of someone's grief, say, by external signs in his behaviour and thus arrive first at the idea of (and belief in) the emotion. This is then converted into an impression and 'acquires such a degree of force and vivacity to become the very passion itself'. It does so via another instance of the principle of association of ideas. Our impression of ourselves has an unparalleled degree of vivacity and is always 'intimately present with us. ... Whatever object, therefore, is related to ourselves must be conceived with a like vivacity of conception, according to the foregoing principles' (Hume 1978: 317).

All other human beings are related to me at least by resemblance and in some cases by contiguity and causation; so when I observe another's grief a share of the unparalleled degree of vivacity present in my impression of myself is communicated to the related idea of his grief; and this idea acquires such a share of vivacity from the supremely lively idea of self as to be converted into an impression, another instance of the passion. If the person whose grief I observe is related to me by contiguity or causation – if he is a neighbour or my child, for example – the relation of resemblance 'receives new force' (Hume 1978: 318) from these other relations, and so the theory predicts that I will be more affected by the plight of friends and family than by that of strangers, as, of course, I am. Thus the operation of sympathy is not impartial, so, although it is essential to the origination of the moral sentiments, in Hume's account, as we shall see it also forces Hume into complications to explain how we correct for sympathy (Hume 1978: 582) in order to achieve a 'general and steady view' (Hume 1978: 581–2) from which moral judgements can be made.

Hume's distinction between calm and violent passions is also relevant to his moral theory, since it is, according to him, because we tend to mistake the influence of the calm passions for the influence of reason that we are tempted to rationalist views of morality. The distinction is a matter of feeling: calm passions produce 'little emotion in the mind' and are 'more known by their effects than the immediate feeling or reaction' (Hume 1978: 417). Contemplating a beautiful garden I feel a sort of calm, unexcited pleasure. But suppose the garden is mine, and I have spent long hours transforming it into its present state. Then my pride may be intense and violent; still more intense, of course, will be my hatred of the vandal who destroys it. It is not clear that the quality that distinguishes violent and calm passions is different from the force and violence that distinguishes ideas from impressions, and how calm passions qualify as impressions. But, just as in the case of ideas and impressions, 'in particular instances they may very nearly approach to each other' (Hume 1978: 2): 'the raptures of poetry and music frequently rise to the greatest height; while those other impressions, properly called passions, may decay into so soft an emotion, as to become in a manner, imperceptible' (Hume 1978: 276). The division has therefore to be made on the basis of what is usual: a passion is to be called violent if its typical instances are violent, calm if its typical instances are calm. 'Moral sentiments count as calm passions, as do benevolence and resentment, the love of life and kindness to children; or the general appetite to good, and aversion to evil, consider'd merely as such' (Hume 1978: 417).

The strength of a passion, its capacity to influence action, is not the same as its degree of violence. A calm passion can be stronger than a violent passion when it has 'become a settled principle of action, and is the predominant inclination of the soul' (Hume 1978: 418–19).

Nevertheless, strength is not wholly independent of violence: 'when we would govern a man, and push him to any action, 'twill commonly be better policy to work upon the violent than the calm passions' (Hume 1978: 419).

Now we need to look at Hume's positive arguments for his anti-rationalism. First we need to consider what Hume means by 'reason' in his argument. Fortunately, he makes this quite clear. As in Book I, Hume uses 'reason' unambiguously to mean our understanding, our inferential faculty, and thus to cover both demonstrative reasoning from ideas and probable reasoning concerning matters of fact. We can therefore anticipate that his discussion in Book III will be about the impotence of (demonstrative and probable) reasoning by itself to provide motives for action.

Hume gives three arguments for his conclusion that 'reason alone can never be a motive to any action of the will' or 'oppose passion in the direction of the will' (Hume 1978: 413).

In the first he distinguishes demonstrative and probable reasoning, and argues that 'neither species of reasoning is the cause of any action'.

Demonstrative reasoning concerns only the world of ideas. The merchant employs arithmetic to work out the total of his debt. If he is not interested in paying his creditors this will have no effect on his actions. Demonstrative reasoning can enable us to work out the means to achieve some prior 'designed end or purpose', but cannot move us to action without some prior purpose. 'Abstract or demonstrative reasoning', Hume concludes, 'never influences our actions, but only as it directs our judgement concerning causes and effects' (Hume 1978: 414).

The same is true, he argues, of probable reasoning, since 'it can never in the least concern us to know, that such objects are causes, and others such effects, if both the causes and effects be indifferent to us' (Hume 1978: 414). We can work out the necessary means to our ends by discovering what causal connections obtain, but unless we have the ends, the discovery will not move us to action.

Hume states this argument in a paragraph that is crucial to the proper interpretation of his thought:

> [W]hen we have the prospect of pain and pleasure from any object, we feel a consequent emotion of aversion and propensity, and are carry'd to avoid or embrace what will give us this uneasiness or satisfaction. ... this emotion rests not here, but ... comprehends whatever objects are connected with its original one by the relation of cause and effect. Here then reasoning takes place to discover this relation. ... But it is evident in this case the impulse arises not from reason but is only directed by it. 'Tis from the prospect of pain or pleasure that the aversion or propensity arises towards any object: And these emotions extend themselves to the causes or effects of that object, as they are pointed out to us by reason and experience.
>
> (Hume 1978: 414)

Hume's picture of motivation thus involves two stages. First, there is a prospect of pain or pleasure, i.e., a belief that some pleasure will result or pain be avoided if certain steps are taken. This produces the emotion of aversion or propensity, and this emotion is extended by means–end reasoning to the causes or effects of that object.

Here we see that Hume dissents from what is sometimes called the 'Humean theory' of motivation, according to which beliefs motivate actions only in the presence of a separate, unmotivated, desire. According to this theory, also sometimes referred to as the belief–desire theory, tracing back the causal history of an action through a person's desires and beliefs we will always eventually trace back to a desire which is not derivative from a belief, but rather conjoins with belief to explain the action.

The passage quoted shows that Hume did not accept the Humean theory of motivation. The prospect of pleasure or pain, which is a belief, arrived at by causal inference, causes us, without any other antecedent desire as input, to feel a consequent emotion, and hence to avoid or embrace what will give us uneasiness or satisfaction. Nor is this passage just a slip on Hume's part. His position is made clear in Book I, in the section 'Of the Influence of Belief', where he gives an additional argument for his account of belief as nothing more than a lively idea. The argument goes as follows. Impressions of pain and pleasure produce passions and motivate actions. Beliefs about future pleasures and pains do the same. If they did not foresight would not enable us to avoid calamities; on the other hand, if all ideas of pleasure and pain had a similar effect we would never enjoy a moment's peace. Thus 'nature has chosen a middle way'. But if beliefs, unlike mere ideas, are similar in their effects to impressions, this can only be because they have more of that quality which distinguishes impressions from mere ideas, that is, greater force and vivacity (Hume 1978: 118–19).

By this argument, the effect of belief on the passions is no more dependent on the existence of prior unmotivated desires than the effect of feelings of pleasure and pain on the passions. Hume's thesis that reason alone never motivates is thus not a thesis about the inefficacy of the products of (demonstrative and probable) reasoning – beliefs – but rather about the inefficacy of the process of reasoning. A creature in which the only causal transitions between perceptions were those of demonstrative and probable reasoning would never have any motive to act.

Hume's second argument for the inertness of reason is a corollary of his first. If reason alone cannot motivate any action it cannot resist passion. Something can oppose a passion only by initiating an impulse to act in the contrary direction. But reason alone cannot initiate any impulse to act. So the apparent conflict between reason and passion has to be differently understood, as, in fact, a conflict within the passions between the calm and the violent.

Hume's third argument for his conclusion, now expressed in the famous dictum 'Reason is, and ought only to be the slave of the passions, and can never pretend to any other office but to serve and obey them', is the infamous 'representation argument':

> A passion is an original existence, or, if you will, modification of existence, and contains not any representative quality, which renders it a copy of any other existence or modification. When I am angry, I am actually possest with the passion, and in that emotion have no more a reference to any other object than when I am thirsty, or sick, or more than five feet high. 'Tis impossible that this passion can be oppos'd by, or be contradictory to truth or reason; since this contradiction consists in the disagreement of ideas, consider'd as copies, with those objects, which they represent.
>
> (Hume 1978: 415)

Hume's argument here can be understood in the light of his distinction between impressions and ideas. Ideas are copies of impressions, or constructed out of copies of impressions, but impressions are not copies of anything. Passions are impressions and therefore not copies. Hume does not have to be interpreted as saying here that passions have no representative content at all, but only that they have no representative content that renders them copies of other existences. Passions have contents and distinct passions have distinct contents, and Hume's theory of the objects and causes of passions is an attempt to explain this (to distinguish my pride in my beautiful garden from my pride in my good looks, and to distinguish the former from the admiration [love] I have towards you because of your landscaping accomplishments). But passions, in Hume's theory, are not capable of being true or false, which he understands as a matter of correspondence between ideas and the external existences they copy. Hume's insight here is one that contemporary philosophers express, for the particular case of the passion of desire, by saying that, unlike belief, desire does not aim at the truth. Beliefs and desires have 'different directions of fit' in relation to the world. Beliefs are mistaken if they do not fit the facts, desires are not mistaken; if I find the world does not fit with my beliefs I must change my beliefs, but if the world does not fit with my desires I can attempt to change the world.

Given that desires, and passions generally, are not capable of truth-value, however, they cannot be conclusions of reasons, 'the discovery of truth and falsehood' (Hume 1978: 458). Thus the conclusion of Hume's representation argument confirms his previous two arguments. He is not denying that beliefs, qua the conclusions of reason, can be the immediate causes of passions, which in turn cause actions. On the contrary, in the case of beliefs about one's own future pleasures and pains, he insists that this can be so; he is only arguing that not every transition in this causal process can be regarded as an instance of reasoning (in the sense he specifies).

He infers that passions cannot, properly speaking, be thought of as reasonable or unreasonable (Hume 1978: 416). We can speak of them as being reasonable or unreasonable 'in a figurative and improper way of speaking', however, in two senses: 'First, when a passion ... is founded on the supposition of the existence of objects, which do not really exist. Secondly, when ... we ... deceive ourselves in our judgment of causes and effects' (Hume 1978: 416).

But when no falsehood thus underlies the exertion of a passion in action, the action cannot be said even in this figurative sense to be unreasonable. Hence:

> The understanding can neither justify nor condemn it. 'Tis not contrary to reason to prefer the destruction of the whole world to the scratching of my finger. 'Tis not contrary to reason for me to chuse my total ruin, to prevent the least uneasiness of an Indian or person wholly unknown to me. 'Tis as little contrary to reason to prefer even my own acknowledg'd lesser good to my greater.
>
> (Hume 1978: 416)

Shocking though this may seem, it follows from Hume's previous reasoning. But it does not mean that someone with the preferences described here is in no way to be criticized. Hume's point is merely that his preferences cannot be in conflict with the conclusions of what he calls reason, whose conclusion is the discovery of truth and falsehood. And it is this sense of 'reason', he thinks, that his rationalist opponents also employ (or should employ).

Hume ends his section 'Of the influencing motives of the will' by appealing to his distinction between calm and violent passions to explain the rationalists' error. Reasoning proceeds without producing any sensible emotion and seldom conveys any pleasure or uneasiness. In this way reasoning is akin to the operation of the calm passions, so the rationalist philosophers, who do 'not examine objects with a strict philosophical eye', and 'judge of things from the first view and appearance' imagine that these actions of mind are entirely the same and confound the calm passions with reason (Hume 1978: 417). Thus a conflict between passion and reason is supposed when the conflict is entirely between two different types of passion.

Reason and morals

Hume's discussion of reason and the passions provides the background to his argument in section I of Part I of Book III of the *Treatise* that moral distinctions are not deriv'd from reason. In fact, much of the section is a recap of the argument just looked at; the rest of the section is devoted to attacks on Clarke, in particular, and culminates in the famous 'modest observation', in which some philosophers have found 'Hume's Law', that no 'ought' can be derived from an 'is'.

Hume begins his *Enquiry* with the question 'Whether 'tis by means of our ideas or impressions we distinguish betwixt vice and virtue, and pronounce an action blameable or praiseworthy' (Hume 1978: 456).

Immediately, he identifies the rationalists with those whose answer to this question is 'By ideas', and proceeds to argue against it.

The identification is justified, given Hume's classificatory system, because reasoning can never have an impression as its conclusion. Thus, neither impressions of sensation, nor, and crucially for Hume's argument here, impressions of reflection, can be conclusions of reason.

The rationalist Hume is attacking maintains a threefold thesis: virtue is nothing more than conformity to reason; it is discoverable by reason; and the recognition of it necessarily influences the will.

Hume's arguments are directed at all three components of this position.

His first argument, the famous 'motivation argument', is briefly stated: 'Morals excite passions, and produce or prevent actions. Reason of itself is utterly impotent in this particular. The rules of morality, therefore, are not conclusions of our reason' (Hume 1978: 457).

The second premise Hume takes from his earlier discussion of reason and the passions. The first is controversial if interpreted as Hume intends it. If it is to play the role he needs it to play it has to mean that morality of itself motivates, that is, motivates independently of any desire one has to be moral, or, for example, to win others' approval. It has to mean that assenting to a moral judgement is intrinsically motivating. But this is something that many philosophers would deny, and Hume's arguments in support of it are hardly conclusive. What he cites as evidence is merely that morals 'naturally ... influence human actions and passions' and 'men are often govern'd by their duties, and are deter'd from some actions by the opinion of injustice, and are impell'd to others by that of obligation' (Hume 1978: 457). But this is consistent with men having either naturally or as a result of their upbringing a desire to act morally, which is additional to their capacity to recognize what is morally right and wrong.

However, though Hume's premise is controversial it is one whose correctness is implied by his own positive account of moral sentiments as impressions of pain and pleasure and, more importantly, it is not something any rationalist of the kind he is concerned to attack could possibly deny.

So, if reason of itself never excites passions or produces or incites actions, and morality of itself does so, does it follow that moral distinctions are not the products of reason alone? It seems that it must follow. But recall what Hume's premise about the motivational inertness of reason comes to. It means that reasoning by itself can never have a passion as a conclusion. Transitions from conclusions of reason to passions are not themselves instances of reasoning. So in a being in whom the only transitions from perceptions to other perceptions are instances of reasoning (whether demonstrative or probable) no such transition could take place. Of course, reason and judgement may be 'the mediate cause of an action, by prompting, or by directing, a passion' (Hume 1978: 462). But a being in whom such transitions take place is not just a rational being. Hume's conclusion, if it is to be seen as following from his premises, is that the capacity for moral discrimination already carries with it the capacity for affections and for those transitions between beliefs and passions and passions and actions that cannot take place in a merely rational being. The capacity for moral discrimination, for recognition of virtue and vice, is not a necessary component of the make-up of every rational being, but founded on the constitution of the human species. Faultlessly rational beings with a different constitution might make quite different moral distinctions from those we make or none at all.

Hume' second argument against the rationalist (Hume 1978: 458) is a repetition of the representation argument from Book III of the *Treatise*: passions, volitions and actions can be neither true nor false, and therefore cannot be either contrary to or conformable to reason.

Hume takes this argument to prove 'directly' that actions do not derive their merits from conformity to reason, since it makes no sense to speak of an action as being 'reasonable' or 'unreasonable', true or false. 'Indirectly' it counts against the rationalist position by supporting the second premise of the motivation argument: reason can never immediately prevent or produce any action by contradicting or approving of it, since actions cannot be the conclusions of reasoning or contradictory to such conclusions.

Hume's third argument is that even if it is allowed that an action may be said to be 'contrary to reason' if it is caused by a passion which rests on a false belief, a person who performs an action which is unreasonable in this 'figurative and improper way of speaking' (Hume 1978: 459) is not usually regarded as morally blameworthy. Hence the rationalist must distinguish those errors ('mistakes of right') that are morally blameworthy from those 'mistakes of fact' that are not. 'But this is to suppose a real right and wrong ... independent of these judgements. A mistake of right may become a species of immorality, but 'tis only a secondary one, and is formed upon some other, antecedent to it' (Hume 1978: 460). Thus it is not truth or falsehood as such which is the source of morals.

Moreover, the rationalist view is inconsistent with the existence of degrees of immorality. If the rightness or wrongness of an action just consists in truth or falsehood (Hume 1978: 460), then the theft of a piece of fruit can be no more reprehensible than the theft of a kingdom.

Hume next turns to the contention that morality, like mathematics, is capable of certainty and demonstration. He draws upon his previous discussion of demonstration in Part III of Book I to reply. The only four relations that depend solely upon ideas and are therefore objects of intuitive or demonstrative knowledge are resemblance, contrariety, degrees in quality and proportions in quantity and number. But all these relations can hold between irrational and even inanimate objects, which cannot be the object of moral evaluation, as well as between actions, passions and volitions; morality therefore cannot 'lie in any of these relations, or the sense of it in their discovery' (Hume 1978: 464).

He illustrates this point, both in the *Treatise* and the moral *Enquiry*, with the crime of parricide: 'A young tree, which overtops and destroys its parent, stands in all the same relations with Nero, when he murdered Agrippina; and if morality consisted merely in relations, would no doubt be equally criminal' (Hume 1975: 293).

Hume's argument might seem weak, and dependent on his peculiar views about demonstration. But he challenges the rationalist to point out some other relation additional to the four he has specified as the ground of demonstration. This new relation, he argues, must satisfy two conditions. First, it must hold only between internal actions and external objects, and never between internal actions alone or external objects alone, for we find morality and immorality only in the actions of mind in relation to external situations (Hume 1978: 465). Second, its perception must necessarily have the same effects on every rational creature. But this second condition is an impossible one, for 'These two particulars are evidently distinct. It is one thing to know virtue and another to conform the will to it' (Hume 1978: 465).

They may be related as cause and effect, but 'It has been shown, in treating of the understanding, that there is no connexion of cause and effect, such as this is suppos'd to be, which is discoverable otherwise than by experience' (Hume 1978: 466).

In short, if the rationalist conception of causation falls, so does the rationalist conception of morality.

Hume claims that these arguments also show that morality does not consist in any 'matter of fact, which can be discovered by the understanding'. He goes on to bolster this conclusion:

> [C]an there be any difficulty in proving, that vice and virtue are not matters of fact, whose existence we can infer by reason? Take any action allow'd to be vicious. ... Examine it in all lights, and see if you can find that matter of fact ... which you call vice. In whichever way you take it you will find only certain passions, motives, volitions and thoughts. There is no other matter of fact in the case. The vice entirely escapes you, as long as you consider the object. You never can find it, till you turn your reflexion into your own breast, and find a sentiment of disapprobation, which arises in you, towards this action. Here is a matter of fact, but 'tis the object of feeling, not of reason. It lies in yourself, not in the object. So that when you pronounce any action or character to be vicious, you mean nothing, but that from the constitution of your nature you have a feeling or sentiment of blame from the contemplation of it. Vice and virtue, therefore, may be compared to sounds, colours, hot and cold, which according to the modern philosophy, are not qualities in object, but perceptions in the mind.

> (Hume 1978: 468–9)

There is no other matter of fact 'in the case', but there is a matter of fact in the mind. This reminds us, of course, of Hume's views on necessary connection. All there is in the world is constant conjunction, but the human mind is so constituted that observation of such a constant conjunction leads to the occurrence of an impression of necessary connection in the mind. Entirely in parallel, according to Hume's view, the 'sentiment of blame', which occurs in the mind on contemplating a vicious action, is an impression of reflection, a passion, which is our human response to the external situation. Consequently, just as Hume gives two definitions of 'cause', so he gives two definitions of 'virtue' or 'personal merit'. 'Personal merit consists altogether in the possession of mental qualities useful or agreeable to the person himself or others' (Hume 1975: 267) and 'virtue [is] whatever mental action or quality gives to a spectator the pleasing sentiment of approbation' (Hume 1975: 289). But what is the source of Hume's confidence that 'there is no other matter of fact in the case', that the vice cannot be found 'in the object'?

It helps to appreciate that what Hume has in mind is not an actual perceptual encounter with a vicious action, but the contemplation of the idea of such an action, perhaps reported in a newspaper. Reading the details of the case we will naturally make a moral evaluation, and in doing so we will be responding to the matters of fact in the case as reported. But precisely because our evaluation of the action is based upon these, the moral value we ascribe to it cannot be another matter of fact in the case, which could not be necessarily connected, by Hume's doctrines, to the others. So in one way, moral values are disanalogous to colours, which depend causally on the primary qualities of their bearers, but can be perceived without any knowledge of their primary qualities. As Hume says in the moral *Enquiry*:

> [I]n moral relations we must be acquainted beforehand with all the objects, and all their relations to each other. ... No new fact to be ascertained; no new relation to be discovered. All the circumstances of the case are supposed to be laid before us, ere we can fix any sentence of blame or approbation.
>
> (Hume 1975: 287)

In this respect moral values are analogous to aesthetic values:

> It is on the proportion, relation and position of all the parts, that all natural beauty depends ... But in all decisions of taste or external beauty, all the relations are beforehand obvious to the eye; and we thence proceed to feel a sentiment of complacency or disgust.
>
> Euclid has fully explained all the qualities of the circle; but he has not in any proposition said a word of its beauty. The reason is evident. The beauty is not a property of the circle. It is only the effect which that figure produces upon the mind, whose peculiar fabric of structure renders it susceptible of such sentiments.
>
> (Hume 1975: 291–2)

Hume concludes section I with the famous afterthought about 'is' and 'ought', that in all systems of morality he has so far encountered, after proceeding in the ordinary way the author suddenly makes a transition from premises linked only by 'is' to a conclusion containing 'ought', which expresses a new relation, a change of the last consequence, since 'it seems altogether inconceivable how this new relation can be a deduction from others which are entirely different from it'. And he adds, 'I ... am persuaded that small attention [to this transition] would subvert all the vulgar systems of morality and let us see, that the distinction of vice and virtue is not founded merely on the relations of objects nor is perceived by reason' (Hume 1978: 470).

This passage has attracted enormous discussion, but it seems clear that it adds nothing but an eloquent summary to what has gone before. Given the generality of Hume's concluding sentence, he cannot mean to be speaking literally only of moral evaluations expressed in sentences containing 'ought' or 'ought not'. Correspondingly, by propositions containing 'is' he must mean all propositions asserting matters of fact that can be discovered by the understanding, however expressible. But, trivially, what is deducible (by the understanding) from a proposition asserting a matter of fact discoverable by the understanding is itself a proposition asserting a matter of fact discoverable by the understanding. If an 'ought' was deducible from an 'is', therefore, Hume's previous arguments would have to be defective. If they are not defective the is/ought paragraph adds nothing new – except, of course, a memorable slogan, worthy of its title 'Hume's Law'.

Morality and sentiment

In section II of the Part I of Book III of the *Treatise*, having to his satisfaction established that virtue and vice are not discoverable by reason, Hume concludes that we make the division between them by 'some impression or sentiment they occasion'. Thus, 'morality is more properly felt than judg'd of' (Hume 1978: 470).

He goes on to raise and briefly answer four questions about the moral sentiments:

1. What are they?
2. How do they affect us?
3. What causes them? and
4. What is the mechanism by which they arise in us?

His answers are: they are particular pleasures and pains; they cause pride and humility, love and hatred; they are caused by the contemplation of human character; and they arise by the operation of the mechanism of sympathy as described in Book II.

That moral sentiments are particular pleasures and pains Hume thinks is sufficiently shown by the fact that the impression arising from virtue is agreeable, that from vice uneasy (Hume 1978: 471). An action is virtuous or vicious because it causes a particular type of pleasure or pain. Nor do we 'infer a character to be virtuous, because it pleases: But in feeling that it pleases after such a particular manner, we in effect feel that it is virtuous' (Hume 1978: 471). Our feeling of pleasure is our moral approbation.

It might be objected that if to be virtuous is just to be a cause of pleasure, 'any object, whether animate or inanimate, rational or irrational, might become morally good ... provided it can excite a satisfaction' (Hume 1978: 471).

But Hume replies, not all pleasures are the same: the pleasure arising from the observation of virtue is different from that arising from the contemplation of an inanimate object (say, a beautiful sunset). Nor are we forced to describe any human action or character as virtuous or vicious just because it pleases or displeases us: 'the good qualities of an enemy are hurtful to us; but may still command our esteem and respect' (Hume 1978: 472). The peculiar pleasures and pains, which denominate an action or character virtuous or vicious, are those that arise 'when the character is considered in general, without reference to our particular interest'. Thus, though it is difficult not to think an enemy vicious, as it may be difficult to acknowledge that the voice of an opponent is agreeable, in both cases the distinction is a real one, and a virtuous character, like a musical voice, 'is nothing but one that naturally gives a particular kind of pleasure'.

Hume's second reply to the objection appeals to the role of the moral sentiments as causes. Unlike other pleasures and pains, by the double relation of impressions and ideas described in Book II, they invariably lead to pride and humility, love and hatred. In this way they are 'clearly distinguishe[d] ... from the pleasure and pain arising from inanimate objects, that often bear no relation to us' (Hume 1978: 473).

The causes of the moral sentiments are therefore certain durable traits of character, which we denominate vices and virtues (as Hume later explains, actions as such are only regarded as virtuous or vicious as signs of vice or virtue). Which qualities of character these are Hume proceeds to discuss in the rest of the *Treatise*. It turns out that the virtues all have at least one of the following four characteristics: they are useful to their possessors, agreeable to their possessors, useful to others, or agreeable to others. The vices, the traits to which we feel disapproval, have a corresponding opposite set of features. (Thus, what Hume calls the 'monkish virtues' – celibacy, fasting penance, mortification, self-denial, humility, silence, solitude – he takes great pleasure in saying, are really vices, despite the 'delusive glosses of superstition and false religion' (Hume 1975: 270).)

The question thus arises, why these traits affect observers in this way? Hutcheson's answer to this question was that virtue (which he identified with benevolence) affected us favourably because we had a moral sense, which was sensitive to this trait. It was, thus, just a basic feature of human nature that human beings find the contemplation of virtue agreeable and that of vice disagreeable. Hume rejects this. His reason is 'for as the number of our duties is, in a manner, infinite, it is impossible that our original instincts should extend to each of them' (Hume 1978: 43). If benevolence were the only virtue, Hutcheson's proposal might be acceptable, but Hume thinks there are many other virtues and that it is necessary to seek a general explanation. His explanation is the mechanism of sympathy. Virtuous traits produce pleasurable feelings in their possessors or others in their circle (either immediately or via their utility). Observers are infected via sympathy by these pleasurable feelings and thus approve of the virtues. So for Hume the virtues are virtues because of their effects, describable in non-moral terms, on their possessors and others in their circle. However, this leaves Hume with a problem, because sympathy varies where moral judgements remain constant. As he says, 'nor can I feel the same lively pleasure from the virtues of a person, who liv'd in Greece two thousand years ago, that I feel from the virtues of a familiar friend and acquaintance. Yet I do not say that I esteem one more than the other' (Hume 1978: 581). Thus Hume's explanatory ambitions create a problem for him that Hutcheson does not have, a problem he tries to solve, as we shall see later, by the introduction of 'the general point of view'.

At this point in the *Treatise*, however, Hume does not draw attention to this problem. Instead he prepares for his classification of virtues into natural and artificial by distinguishing senses of 'natural'. If 'nature' is opposed to artifice, he concludes, 'it may be disputed whether the notion of virtue be natural or not', and he adds, 'perhaps it will appear afterwards', as, of course, it does 'that our sense of some virtues is artificial and that of others natural' (Hume 1978: 474).

The virtues

The distinction between natural and artificial virtues is introduced in section I of Part II of Book III of the *Treatise*. Artificial virtues are those that produce pleasure and approbation by means of an artifice or contrivance, which arises from the circumstances and necessities of mankind (Hume 1978: 477). Natural virtues are in no way dependent upon convention. Justice is Hume's prime example of an artificial virtue, benevolence his prime example of a natural virtue.

In more detail the distinction is this. Natural virtues are original parts of human nature and present in human beings whether in society or out of it. They are useful or agreeable, either to their possessors or to those in their possessors' circle, on each occasion they are manifested, and because of this they produce in a spectator the pleasing sentiment of approbation whenever observed and are thus constituted virtues. Artificial virtues, by contrast, are not original parts of human nature. They are not present in human beings in their natural state outside of a society. They develop as human inventions, as solutions to problems self-interested human beings face, given their natural capacities, natural dispositions (including those constituting the natural virtues) and contingent circumstances. Their exercise is not always useful or agreeable to anyone, considered individually, but their existence as general dispositions of human beings in society is necessary to the existence of any society at all. Our approval of these comes about via the same mechanism as our approval of the natural virtues, but in this case it is their general utility as society-wide practices to which spectators respond in approving of them.

In the *Treatise* Hume discusses the artificial virtues first and is concerned with two questions: How do they come to be? And how do they come to qualify as virtues? In the moral *Enquiry* he does not explicitly use the terminology of artificial and natural virtues (though his views do not seem very different in content from those in the *Treatise*) and he first discusses benevolence (a natural virtue) before discussing (the artificial virtue of) justice.

We shall look at what he says about the natural virtues before turning to the artificial virtues.

The chief interest of Hume's discussion of the natural virtues is that it demonstrates his opposition to any form of egoism in morality. He refers to this view as 'the selfish theory' and regards it as deeply sceptical (unlike his own position) and as denying the reality of moral distinctions. He attacks it in the moral *Enquiry* with arguments based on the existence of the natural virtues and the fact that we approve of them. He does not deny that we have selfish motives and that our generosity to others is limited, and partial, but he insists that selfishness is not the whole story, as both empirically observable facts and theoretical considerations dictate.

The basic objection to the selfish theory is we can morally approve of what is not in any way related to our own interests:

> We frequently bestow praise on virtuous actions, performed in distant ages and countries. A generous ... deed performed by an adversary, commands our approbation; though prejudicial to our particular interest. ... Where private advantage concurs with general affection for virtue, ... these distinct sentiments ... have a very different feeling and influence on the mind.

(Hume 1975: 215–16)

Such examples suffice, Hume thinks, to refute one version of the selfish hypothesis (associated with Mandeville) 'that all benevolence is mere hypocrisy, friendship a cheat, public spirit a farce' (Hume 1975: 295). However, he distinguishes another version of the selfish hypothesis, which he does not dismiss so abruptly, and associates with Hobbes, Locke and Epicurus. According to this version we do not consciously pursue only our self-interest, nevertheless there is no passion that is not self-interested: 'unknown to ourselves we seek our own gratification while we appear the most deeply engaged in schemes for the liberty and happiness of mankind' (Hume 1975: 295).

But even as a speculative hypothesis, Hume thinks, this Hobbist view should be rejected. For its only purported advantage is the greater explanatory simplicity it claims to offer by substituting one principle of human nature for several. But, Hume thinks, the appeal to simplicity is implausible. The cases to be explained away by the Hobbist are just too many:

> [A] man who grieves for a valued friend, who needed his patronage and protection ... animals ... susceptible to kindness to their own species and to ours ... a fond mother who loses her health by assiduous attention to her sick child and afterwards dies of grief when

freed by its death from the slavery of that attendance ... desire for the welfare of a friend, even though absence or death should prevent our participation in it.

(Hume 1975: 299–300)

Anyway, Hume argues, borrowing now from Butler, the hypothesis that allows of a disinterested benevolence is actually the simpler. Here he appeals to the existence of the direct passions noted in section IX of Part III of Book II of the *Treatise* (Hume 1978: 439), which produce good and evil rather than proceed from them: 'There are bodily appetites which necessarily precede all sensual enjoyment and carry us directly to seek possession of their object. Thus hunger and thirst have food and drink for their end' (Hume 1975: 301). I get pleasure from the satisfaction of these desires, but if I did not have them such pleasures would not be possible. Pursuit of the pleasures of food and drink is therefore secondary to such natural appetites and is constitutive of my self-interest only because they exist. The same is true, as Hume stresses elsewhere, of sexual pleasure. Additionally, there are 'mental passions, such as fame or power or vengeance by which we are immediately impelled to seek particular objects without any regard to interest'. Again, I can take pleasure in the satisfaction of these ends and can pursue that pleasure as a part of my own happiness or self-interest only 'when once is it constituted such by our original affections'. If I were indifferent to food, to drink and sex, cared nothing for what people thought of me, and had no ambition or feelings of resentment or anger towards others who wronged me, there would be little meaning to talk of my self-interest.

But Hume now concludes:

Where is the difficulty in conceiving that this may likewise be the case with benevolence and friendship, and that, from the original frame of our temper, we may feel a desire of another's happiness or good, which by means of that affection, becomes our own good, and is afterwards pursued, from the combined motives of benevolence and self-enjoyment? ... vengeance, from the force alone of passion, may be so eagerly pursued, as to make us knowingly neglect every consideration of ease, interest or safety ... what a malignant philosophy must it be, that will not allow, to humanity and friendship, the same privileges, which are indisputably granted to ... enmity and resentment?

(Hume 1975: 302)

We can now return to Hume's discussion of the artificial virtues – justice, or honesty with respect to property, fidelity to promises, allegiance to magistrates, conformity to the laws of nations, chastity and modesty (in women). In the case of all of these the difficulty Hume sees is that it is not true in every single instance that the virtuous act is either useful or agreeable to the agent or others. If I repay a debt to a miser or an alcoholic, who will hide it away or waste it on drink, instead of using the money to help the needy, no one's interest is served, yet repaying the debt is required if I am honest. The case is the same for all the other artificial virtues. So Hume faces two questions. How do these virtues come into existence? And how do they come to be objects of moral approval?

Hume explains the difficulty the artificial virtues pose for him in section I of Part II of Book III of the *Treatise*, in which he argues that justice cannot be a natural virtue.

The starting point of his argument is the plausible claim that the moral merit of an action derives from its motive (Hume 1978: 478). Consequently, 'that no action can be virtuous, or morally good, unless there be in human nature some motive to produce it, distinct from the sense of its morality' (Hume 1978: 478).

Of course, there is a sense in which the sense of morality or duty may be said to motivate action on its own, when we do something solely because we think that it is the right thing to do, and Hume offers an explanation:

When any virtuous motive or principle is common in human nature, a person who feels his heart devoid of that motive, may hate himself upon that account, and may perform the action without the motive, from a certain sense of duty, in order to acquire by practice, that virtuous principle, or at least, to disguise to himself, as much as possible, his want of it.

(Hume 1978: 479)

But to act in this way is not to aim, unintelligibly, at performing an action which is motivated by some virtuous motive or other; it is to aim to produce in oneself a virtuous motive as a habit, or: to make it less obvious to oneself that one lacks it and so to lessen one's painful self-hatred. But these motives, as Hume says, 'suppose in human nature some distinct principles, which are capable of producing the action, and whose moral beauty renders the action meritorious' (Hume 1978: 479).

Turning now to justice, Hume asks, suppose I borrow some money, what motive have I to repay it?

Of course, the answer is that it is the honest thing to do. But Hume objects: though this motive is a perfectly intelligible one to man in his civilized state, outside society, in the absence of conventions, it is perfectly unintelligible, because a man in such a state does not have the concept, or idea, of honesty or respect for property, because he does not have the concept, or idea, of property. So he cannot have the motive of respect for property. As he says later, only when a 'convention, concerning abstinence from the possessions of others, is enter'd into, and every one has acquir'd a stability in his possessions, [does] there immediately [arise] the ideas of justice and injustice; as also those of property, right and obligation' (Hume 1978: 491).

So what motives that already exist in a state of nature could motivate repayment? Hume considers three candidates: self-love, public benevolence or regard for the public interest and private benevolence or concern for another individual. He quickly shows that none will do. Self-love, when it acts at liberty, is plainly opposed to honesty and 'the source of all injustice and violence' (Hume 1978: 480). Not all just actions, considered individually, are in the public interest and the public interest is not relevant if the loan is secret, though the duty to repay the loan remains. Anyway, concern for the public interest would be a motive 'too remote and too sublime to affect the generality of mankind' (Hume 1978: 481). Moreover, there is in fact no such passion in human minds as public benevolence, or regard to the interests of mankind, merely as such. We are affected by the sufferings of others via sympathy, but this extends beyond our species and is variable within it. As for private benevolence, it cannot explain why I should repay the loan even if my creditor 'is a profligate debauchee, and would rather receive harm than benefit from large possessions' (Hume 1978: 482). In short, because the honest action is sometimes one that is in no one's interest, none of the natural virtues Hume considers can provide the necessary motive in every case in which we think an obligation to repay a debt exists. Hume concludes that we must 'allow that a sense of justice and injustice is not deriv'd from nature, but arises artificially, tho' necessarily, from education and human conventions' (Hume 1978: 483).

His next task is to explain how this comes about.

According to Hume's story it does so as a remedy which nature provides 'in the judgement and understanding, for what is irregular and incommodious in the affections' (Hume 1978: 481). Given their selfishness and confined generosity (which is consistent with their possession of all the natural virtues) men are supposed to see, as a result of their experience in the biological family unit, in which cooperation takes place without any convention and provides an illustration of the advantages to be gained by working together, that it is in their interest and that of their loved ones to form the intention to leave to others their possessions so long as they themselves are left theirs.

Each indicates to the others this awareness and so each comes to be aware that the others are aware of the advantages of cooperation. Each then forms the conditional intention or 'resolution': to refrain from taking the possessions of another (i.e., the goods they have acquired through labour or fortune) provided he refrains from mine, and each acts on that intention. Thus a convention or agreement arises, pace Hobbes and Locke, 'without the interposition of a promise; since the actions of each of us have a reference to those of the other, and are performed upon the supposition, that something is to be performed on the other part'. In the same way, 'Two men, who pull the oars of a boat do it by agreement or convention, tho' they have never given promises to each other' (Hume 1978: 490).

This convention now provides the basis for defining the notions of justice and property. A man acts justly if the motive for his action is the conditional intention just identified (it is this conditional intention which is the real and universal motive for obeying the laws of equity (Hume 1978: 483), which we do not have naturally. One's property consists of those goods that will be left in one's possession in a society of just men. Thus the origin of justice explains that of property. The same artifice gives rise to both.

Hume elaborates this story to explain how the institutions of promise and government arise. But the elaborations are less important than the starting point. Briefly, promising and the obligation to honour promises arises because of our interest in cooperating in activities where the two parties cannot act simultaneously. Thus it is advantageous for all of us that there be a form of words whereby we can signal to others that we will do our part later, and not be trusted to cooperate again if we fail. When someone utters this form of words, he 'subjects himself to the penalty of never being trusted again in the case of failure' (Hume 1978: 522). Why make a promise then? Because out of self-interest one recognizes that it is to one's advantage to show willingness to cooperate in non-simultaneous actions. And why fulfil a promise once given? Because out of self-interest one recognizes that it is to one's advantage to retain the willingness of others to cooperate.

Government arises because when society grows too large men cease to see that their self-interest is served by just action (though, Hume thinks, it still is), and favour their short-term interests. Instituting government, and, in particular, appointing magistrates to enforce the rules of justice, brings short-term interest in line with long-term interest. People agree to appoint magistrates, foreseeing that in the future they will be tempted to act unjustly, influenced by short-term interest, in order to ensure that when the time comes to act their short-term interest in avoiding punishment by the magistrates will require them to act justly.

By similar processes self-interest and confined generosity lead to the development of the institution of marriage and the laws between nations.

But so far Hume has not explained why we regard acting in accordance with the rules of these institutions as virtuous. Why, fundamentally, do we annexe the idea of virtue to justice and vice to injustice (Hume 1978: 498). To explain this is to explain the moral obligation to justice, or the sentiment of right and wrong.

Hume's explanation is again via the notion of sympathy. As society grows larger, men do not readily perceive that their self-interest lies in acting justly and that 'disorder and confusion follow upon *every* breach of the rules' (Hume 1978: 499), and frequent violations of the rules occur. But even when the injustice is so distant that it in no way affects their interests men are displeased by injustice, since they sympathize with its victims, consider it as prejudicial to human society, and pernicious to every one that approaches the person guilty of it. The artifice of politicians and private education and instruction also add to the motivational force of the sense of justice. But, Hume insists, they are merely supplementary: this progress of sentiments is natural and even necessary (Hume 1978: 500).

In the *Treatise* Hume appears to believe that there can be no real conflict between self-interest, properly perceived, and acting justly, for 'disorder and confusion follow upon every breach of the rule' (Hume 1978: 499). However, this seems evidently false, and in the moral *Enquiry*, at least, he acknowledges this, introducing the figure of 'the selfish knave':

> A man, taking things in a certain light, may often seem to be a loser by his integrity. ... though ... without a regard to property, no society could subsist; yet ... a sensible knave, in particular incidents, may think that an act of iniquity or infidelity will make a considerable addition to his fortune, without causing any considerable breach in the social union and confederacy. That honesty is the best policy, may be a good general rule; but it is liable to many exceptions; And he, it may perhaps be thought, conducts himself with most wisdom, who observes the general rule, and takes advantage of the exceptions.
>
> (Hume 1975: 282)

The problem is not that the sensible knave cannot be proved to be irrational. A man who lacks the natural virtues of benevolence and gratitude need not be any less rational than one endowed with those virtues; but the possibility of such a man is of no concern to

Hume. The problem the sensible knave poses is rather a challenge to Hume's rational reconstruction of the origin of the artificial virtue of justice. As we saw, men are supposed to see, as a result of their experience in the biological family unit, that it is in their interest and that of their loved ones to form the intention to leave to others their possessions so long as they themselves are left theirs. But what the possibility of the sensible knave shows is that this supposed insight is no such thing; conforming to such a general conditional intention will not always be in the interest of men endowed with the natural dispositions Hume supposes. Since it is not true that it is in the best interests of men to conform to such a resolution, it cannot be the remedy which nature provides 'in the judgement and understanding' (i.e., our reasoning faculty working correctly) for the defects in our affections Hume describes. In the *Treatise* Hume does not confront this problem because he thinks, or at least, says, that 'disorder and confusion follows upon *every* breach of the rules' (my emphasis) and

> [H]owever single acts of justice may be contrary, either to public or private interest, 'tis certain, that the whole plan ... is highly conducive ... to the well-being of every individual. 'Tis impossible to separate the good from the ill. ... And even every individual person must find himself a gainer, on balancing the account; since, without justice, society must immediately dissolve.

(Hume 1978: 497)

In the *Enquiry* he recognizes that this is not so. His response to the sensible knave is to say: 'If a man think, that this reasoning much requires an answer, it will be a little difficult to find any ...'. He adds: 'If his heart rebels not against such pernicious maxims. ... he has indeed lost a considerable motive to virtue, and we may expect that his practice is answerable to his speculation' (Hume 1975: 283).

In truth, this is no answer. Hume's account of the origin of justice in the *Treatise* therefore fails. And the same, we can now see, is true of his account, via sympathy, of our coming to annexe the idea of virtue to justice. For there may be no victims to sympathize with in particular cases, and no advantage to society as a whole from the just act. Hume describes such a case. I encounter: 'Two person, who dispute for an estate; of whom one is rich, a fool and a batchelor; the other poor, a man of sense and has a numerous family: The first is my enemy; the second my friend' (Hume 1978: 532).

In this case, if I am 'actuated only by natural motives, without any combination or convention with others', then 'whether I be actuated in this affair by public or private interest, by friendship or enmity, I must do my utmost to procure the estate to the latter' (Hume 1978: 532). And sympathy will not lead a spectator to disapprove of my so acting unless he falsely believes that in doing so I am manifesting a disposition 'prejudicial to human society and pernicious to every one that approaches the person guilty of it' (Hume 1978: 498).

The correction of our sentiments

We can now turn to a final complication. The moral sentiments are the foundation of Hume's moral theory, and they are produced via the mechanism of sympathy. The pleasant and unpleasant feelings produced via such sympathy are distinct from those that arise from our particular interest, so we are able, with temper and judgement, to distinguish in an enemy 'his opposition to our interest and real villainy or baseness' (Hume 1978: 472).' 'Tis only when a character is considered in general, without reference to our particular interest, that it causes such a feeling or sentiment, as denominates it particularly good or evil' (Hume 1978: 472).

Nevertheless, although the effects of sympathy are independent of our own particular interest, they are still variable across time and persons in ways that moral judgements are not. Hume perceives this variability as an objection to his account that needs an answer:

[A]s this sympathy is very variable, it may be thought, that our sentiments of morals must admit of all the same variations. ... But we give the same approbation to the moral qualities in China as in England. They appear equally virtuous, and recommend themselves equally to the esteem of a judicious spectator. The sympathy varies without a variation in our esteem. Our esteem proceeds, therefore, not from sympathy.

(Hume 1978: 581)

In short, how I feel about a person will vary depending on his contiguity and resemblance to me; but we have a system of evaluation embodied in our moral discourse that discounts such differences (as when I am able to recognize the greater virtue of Marcus Brutus compared to my much-loved diligent and faithful servant [Hume 1978: 528]). The challenge Hume sees is to provide an explanation of this system of moral evaluation in the framework of his sympathy-based account.

His response is to introduce the notions of a general point of view and the correction of sentiments:

> ['T]is impossible we could ever converse together on reasonable terms, were each of us to consider characters and persons, only as they appear from his peculiar point of view. In order, therefore, to prevent these continual contradictions, and arrive at a more stable judgement of things, we fix on some steady and general points of view; and always in our thoughts place ourselves in them, whatever may be our present situation. In like manner, external beauty is determined merely by pleasure, and a beautiful countenance cannot give so much pleasure, at a distance of twenty paces, as when brought nearer to us. We say not, however, that it appears less beautiful: Because we know what effect it will have in such a position, and by that reflexion we correct its momentary appearance.
>
> (Hume 1978: 581–2)

We distinguish between how things seem and how they are in the case of beauty, by appeal to how they would seem from a certain point of view – not too far away and not too near. And, Hume thinks, the moral situation is precisely analogous. In fact, the situation is precisely analogous in all cases in which we distinguish between reality and appearance, which is why he speaks in the passage quoted of 'general points of view' in the plural:

> All objects seem to diminish by their distance, yet we do not say, that they actually diminish; but correcting the appearance by reflexion, arrive at a more constant and establish'd judgement concerning them.
>
> (Hume 1978: 602)

In the case of morality, we arrive at this more constant and established judgement and correct our sentiments by 'confining our view to that narrow circle in which a man moves, in order to form a judgement of his moral character' (Hume 1978: 602). Thus we can judge Marcus Brutus more laudable than our servant because 'we know that, were we to approach near to that renown'd patriot, he would command a much higher degree of affection and admiration' (Hume 1978: 528).

In this way, Hume thinks, a sympathy-based account of moral judgement is consistent with and can explain the relative invari-ability of our moral judgements. Just as we judge a statue to be beautiful, or a mountain enormous, even though it appears differ-ently to different people or the same person at different times, so can we judge a man to be virtuous even if people placed at differ-ent sympathetic distances from him and his circle find different sentiments aroused in them by contemplation of his character.

The moral case is different, of course, in that no change, in, say, the size the mountain appears to me to have can come about with-out an actual change of my position relative to it; but in the moral case I can change my sympathetic distance merely by reflection and come to have towards Marcus Brutus the sentiments a member of his narrow circle would have had. However, although this is pos-sible, Hume thinks, it is not at all common, nor do our passions often correspond entirely to the present theory (Hume 1978: 582).

What does correspond is our language, which we correct, though the sentiments are more stubborn and unalterable (Hume 1978: 582). Thus, though the passions do not always follow our corrections, these corrections serve sufficiently to regulate our abstract notions (Hume 1978: 585) and this is 'sufficient for dis-course, and ... all our purposes in company and in the schools' (Hume 1978: 603).

Another area in which first sight Hume's theory seems wanting is that of 'virtue in rags':

> Virtue in rags is still virtue; and the love which it procures, attends
> a man into a dungeon or desert, where the virtues can no longer be
> exerted in action. ... Now ... if sympathy were the source of our

esteem for virtue, that sentiment of approbation cou'd only take place, when the virtue actually attained its end.

(Hume 1978: 584)

Hume's reply is:

[A] man whose limbs promise strength and activity, is esteem'd handsome, tho' condemned to perpetual captivity. The imagination has a set of passions belonging to it, on which our sentiments of beauty much depend ... Where character is, in every respect, fitted to be beneficial to society, the imagination passes from the cause to the effect, [though] there are still some circumstances wanting to render the cause a compleat one. General rules create a species of probability, which sometimes influences the judgement, and always the imagination.

But he acknowledges that when the cause is complete it gives a stronger pleasure to the spectator. Yet we do not say that it is more virtuous. As in the case of the correction of our sentiments to discount for different sympathetic distances, our language is affected more than our passions, and this, Hume thinks, is in accordance with what we actually know to be the case: 'our heart does not always take part with these general notions', even though, ' they are sufficient for discourse, and serve all our purposes in company, in the pulpit, on the theatre, and in the schools' (Hume 1978: 603).

We say that a character is virtuous therefore when we ignore our particular sympathetic distance from it and judge that it has 'a tendency to the advantage of those who have any immediate connexion or intercourse with the person possessed of it' (Hume 1978: 602–3). We say that a character is vicious when we ignore our particular sympathetic distance and judge that it has a tendency disadvantageous to those who have any immediate connexion or intercourse with the person possessed of it. These are the circumstances in which we make these pronouncements. But what do we mean by them? What are we saying when we call a character trait a virtue (or a vice)? Hume gives two definitions of virtue. But neither definition is wholly satisfactory, since neither exhausts what is going on when a character is pronounced to be

virtuous; 'we spread our minds on the world', as in the case of causation, we say, or attempt to say, something that could not possibly
be true, 'gilding or staining all natural objects with the colours
borrowed from internal sentiment' (Hume 1975: 294). Thus, in
the end, in our thought about virtue and vice, as in our thought
about causes and effects, Hume seems to want to say, we go beyond
what is intelligible. There are thoughts about the utility and agree-
ableness of character traits to their possessors or their possessors'
circle, and there are thoughts about the effects such traits have on
sympathetic spectators. But there are no genuine further thoughts
we can achieve by 'spreading our minds on the world'. There is
only 'confusion and obscurity' (Hume 1978: 238).

Chapter Seven

Religion

Introduction

Hume's main writings on religion include two sections of the *Enquiry Concerning Human Understanding* – 'Of miracles' and 'Of a particular providence and a future state' – his short book *The Natural History of Religion* (Hume 1998) and his posthumously published *Dialogues Concerning Natural Religion* (Hume 1998). Various essays and letters are also significant, particularly his provocative essays 'On Suicide' and 'On the Immortality of the Soul', originally intended to be published with the *Natural History*. In these writings Hume's rejection of Christianity, both Catholic and Protestant, is evident. His own position is less evident. James Boswell reports that Hume told him that he had never entertained any belief in religion since he began to read Locke and Clarke (Boswell 1947: 76). And it is clear from 'On the immortality of the soul' that Hume had no belief in a Christian hereafter. On the other hand he refused to call himself an atheist or deist, and repeatedly affirmed the existence of God in his writings. In the Appendix to the *Treatise* a footnote reads: 'the order of the universe proves an omnipotent mind. ... Nothing more is requisite to give a foundation to all the articles of religion' (Hume 1978: 633). In the Introduction to the *Natural*

History of Religion he writes: 'the whole frame of nature bespeaks an intelligent author; and no rational enquirer can, after serious reflection, suspend his belief a moment with regard to the principles of genuine Theism and Religion' (Hume 1998: 134). In the *Dialogues* Demea and, more significantly, Philo, accept that the existence, if not the nature, of God is indubitable, and even in the final section Philo, the sceptic and critic of the main arguments for the existence of God, avows that 'no one pays more profound adoration to the divine being, as he discovers himself to reason' (Hume 1998: 116).

Certainly much of this is insincere. Open expressions of doubt or denial of religion, and, in particular, of Christianity, were not possible for a prudent man of Hume's time. As it was, Hume's irreligious reputation lost him two university chairs; he had to suppress the essays on suicide and immortality originally intended for publication with the *Natural History* on threat of prosecution; and he thought it best to reserve the *Dialogues* for posthumous publication. He therefore wrote about religion with the greatest artfulness and concealment. Nevertheless, most scholars find it hard to deny some semblance of religious belief in Hume – or, at least, some reluctance to deny outright the existence of any sort of divine being. And, in fact, in what was Hume's last word on the subject, a passage added to the final speech of Philo in the final section of the *Dialogues* in the final months of Hume's life, we find the following affirmation:

> If the whole of natural theology ... resolves itself into one simple, though somewhat ambiguous, at least undefined proposition, that the cause or causes of order in the universe probably bear some remote analogy to human intelligence ... what can the most inquisitive, contemplative, and religious man do more than give a plain philosophical assent to the proposition ... and believe that the arguments on which it is established, exceed the objections which lie against it.

(Hume 1998: 129)

Determining what this amounts to is the key to resolving the enigma of Hume on religion.

It is helpful to compare his examination of religious belief with his examinations in Part IV of Book I of the *Treatise* of belief in an external world and an enduring self. In both the latter cases, as we have seen, Hume distinguishes two questions, an epistemological one and a psychological one. The epistemological question is about the reasons or justification we have for the belief; the psychological one is about its causes. In both cases Hume concludes that the epistemological question has no good answer and answers the psychological question by giving an account of its genesis by appeal to features of the mere imagination.

Hume's discussion of religious belief follows the same pattern. He distinguishes between (primitive) polytheism and (sophisticated) monotheism, and argues in the *Natural History* that, as a matter of historical fact, the latter arises from the former, not as a reasoned development, but as a result of the processes of the imagination he there details. He makes it evident that he, of course, thinks polytheism itself an absurd and inconsistent doctrine, which has no basis in reason but arises only from man's fearful imagination. But monotheism, at least in the form of the Christian belief in a divine personal creator of the world who continues to sustain it and work within it, and is almighty and all-good, he argues, not only does not have a rational origin, but cannot be defended by rational arguments, and in fact, is most reasonably regarded as false. The case for the proposition that monotheism cannot be defended by rational arguments is presented in 'Of miracles' and in the *Dialogues* (anticipated by 'On a particular providence and a future state'). The argument that Christian monotheism is actually contrary to reason also occurs in the *Dialogues*, in Hume's discussion of the problem of evil, where, speaking through Philo, he makes it plain that even if evil is consistent with the existence of the beneficent Christian deity, given the evil there is in the world it is impossible rationally to appeal to features of the world as support for monotheism; rather, to anyone who starts from his experience of the world, the only 'true conclusion is, the original source of all things is entirely indifferent to all these principles and has no more regard to good above ill than to heat above cold' (Hume 1998: 114).

Despite the parallels between Hume's discussion of belief in an external world and the self and belief in a divine being one very important difference remains. Though he thinks belief in an external world and self to be false, or at least, contrary to reason, he also thinks it inevitable. Not so for belief in the divine. Hume does not think it is universal and ascribes its origin in the *Natural History* to 'secondary causes', which may in some cases not operate at all (Hume 1998: 135).

As regards reasons for (as opposed to causes of) of religious belief, Hume followed tradition in distinguishing between those provided by natural religion (or natural theology, as it is now more frequently called), and those provided by revelation. Natural religion consists of arguments for the existence of God (or the gods) that are available to any intelligent reasoner from his experience of the world. Revelation is the body of truths about his existence and nature that God has conveyed through his divinely inspired scriptures and messengers. That the world is a product of intelligent design, for example, was taken by eighteenth century theists, and by Hume, as a conclusion of natural religion; that the son of God was made man in first century Palestine, or that we can expect life eternal in the form of resurrection, were taken to be truths revealed truths in the Bible. Christians accepted that an answer was required to the question why the particular revelation contained in the New Testament should be accepted as genuine, as divinely inspired rather than a product of human invention – as they thought was true, for example, of the Qur'an. Their answer was that the revelation of Christianity was certified by the miracles and (miraculously) fulfilled prophecies recorded in the New Testament, most importantly, the resurrection of Jesus Christ. Only God could bring about miracles and therefore it was rational to believe in the divine origin of the writings in which such miracles were recorded.

Thus, as Hume saw it, there were two possible kinds of rational ground for Christian belief: natural religion and miraculously certified revelation. He therefore attacks on two fronts. In 'Of miracles' he argues that, leaving the possible conclusions of natural religion aside, 'no human testimony can have such force as to prove a miracle, and to make it a just foundation for any ... system of religion' (Hume 1975: 137). Revelation, by itself, therefore, cannot provide rational ground for Christian belief. Hume attacks the conclusions of natural religion in the section of the *Enquiry* following the section on miracles, and more extensively in the *Dialogues*, where Philo's last word on natural religion (in the last paragraph added before Hume's death) is: 'A person, seasoned with a just sense of the imperfections of natural reason, will fly to revealed truth with the greatest avidity. ... To be a philosophical sceptic, is, in a man of letters, the first and most essential step towards being a sound believing Christian' (Hume 1998: 129).

This is disingenuous, but the innocent Christian, not having read 'Of miracles' will not know it. Hume attacks on two fronts, but he does not attack natural religion and revelation at the same time, and he does not advertise one attack when conducting the other.

The reason for this artfulness is that Hume wants his writings on religion to be read by and to persuade the religiously inclined. His aim is to undermine the elements of their belief system piece by piece so that his arguments will not be recognized until it is too late (after they have been read and allowed to take hold of the mind) as parts of the comprehensive critique of Christian belief they constitute.

We can now turn to details.

Miracles

'Of miracles' is still a subject of controversy (Fogelin 2003; Earman 2000). It is disputed what its conclusions are, whether its arguments are effective, whether it is original, and how it can be reconciled with Hume's general philosophical scheme.

We can begin with the last issue. In broad outline Hume's argument is that since miracles are by definition at least highly improbable occurrences, opposed to our uniform experience of the course of nature, we need very good reason to believe someone who testifies to a miracle, since 'a wise man proportions his belief to the evidence'. But there never has been a sufficiently good reason to accept such testimony, and given the special features of testimony associated with religious miracles, there never could be sufficiently good reason to accept testimony to such a miracle.

However, it has seemed to some writers – for example, C. D. Broad (1916–17) and C. S. Lewis (1947) – that Hume's scepticism about induction precludes his arguing in this way. To accept that a miracle has occurred is indeed to accept that the course of nature has changed. But we have no reason on the sceptical Humean view to think that the course of nature will not change: the belief that it will not change has no more rational support than the belief that it will; as far as the competition for degrees of reasonableness is concerned, these beliefs (like all possible beliefs about the unobserved) are tied for last place (Stroud 1977: 54). Belief in miracles on the basis of testimony is no more unjustified than disbelief in them on the basis of their conflict with past experience. In short, Hume's demand for a justification for belief in miracles, in particular, is an inconsistency in his philosophy.

If Hume were an inductive sceptic Broad and Lewis would be right. We have seen, however, good reason to reject this interpretation of Hume. 'Of miracles' is better seen as further evidence against the interpretation of Hume as a sceptic about induction, and evidence for the literalist interpretation given in chapter 3, than as a proof of Hume's inconsistency. And, as we shall now see, the distinctions Hume makes in the context of his account of the 'reasonable foundations of belief and opinion' (Hume 1978: 143) in sections XI–XIII of Part III of Book I of the *Treatise* are crucial to his discussion of miracles. (It appears likely, in fact, that it was after these sections of the *Treatise* that Hume originally intended the discussion of miracles to be placed, before he decided to omit it from the *Treatise*.)

'Of miracles' is divided into two parts, conventionally, but misleadingly, referred to as the a priori argument against miracles and the a posteriori argument against miracles. The conclusion of Part 1, based on general arguments about testimony and evidence, is that

> [N]o testimony is sufficient to establish a miracle, unless the testimony be of such a kind, that its falsehood would be more miraculous, than the fact, which it endeavours to establish: And even in that case there is a mutual destruction of arguments, and

the superior only gives us an assurance suitable to that degree of force, which remains after deducting the inferior.

(Hume 1975: 115–16)

Note that this is a merely conditional conclusion ('unless'). In Part 2, appealing to a mixed bag of empirical and a priori arguments, Hume aims to establish two conclusions: (1) that there never was a miraculous event established on so full an evidence (as to constitute a proof), and (2) that no human testimony can ever have such force as to prove a miracle, and make it a just foundation for any ... system of religion (Hume 1975: 116, 127).

In Part 1 Hume begins by emphasizing the fallibility of reasoning concerning matters of fact. Where past experience is uniform we expect it to continue with the highest certainty, but where it is variable we rest less confidence in it. Thus 'a wise man proportions his belief to the evidence'. Hume goes on to explain how, using language familiar from the earlier part of the *Enquiry* and the *Treatise*, Book I.

In ... conclusions ... founded on infallible experience, he expects the event with the last degree of assurance, and regards his past experience as a full proof of [its] future existence. . . .. In other cases ... he weighs the opposite experiments. ... and when at last he fixes his judgment the evidence exceeds not what he calls probability. All probability, then, supposes an opposition of experiments and observations; where the one side is found to overbalance the other and to prove a degree of evidence proportional to the superiority.

(Hume 1975: 110–11)

A key contrast of which Hume reminds his readers here is that between proofs and probabilities, a distinction which he makes to conform himself to common discourse (Hume 1978: 124). What is proven can still be false – though I have no doubt that the sun will rise tomorrow and so must regard my experience as a proof, I still, in Hume's terminology, do not know it, since the course of nature might change. And if it did I would then be justified in denying what I now take to be proven. In Part 2 Hume actually describes a circumstance in which it would be rational to reject something of which we now have a proof (and accept the occurrence of a miracle).

Hume now applies this distinction to the particular case of testimony, noting its importance, but emphasizing that its veracity cannot just be assumed:

> It being a general maxim, that no objects have any discoverable connexion together and that all inferences ... are founded merely on the experience of ... constant ... conjunction: it is evident that we ought not to make an exception to this maxim in favour of human testimony, whose connexion with any event seems as little necessary as any other.
>
> (Hume 1975: 111)

My testimony to an event is one thing; the event is another. There are no necessary connections between distinct existences, so only experience can provide any reason for thinking that, given the testimony, the event testified about must have occurred. And, of course, we know that men lie, are deceived, and misremember, so it is not reasonable to accept just any piece of testimony without question.

Hume goes on to describe the circumstances of testimony which should make us doubt it: if the character of the witnesses is doubtful; if they are too few; if they deliver their testimony in a suspicious manner; if they are interested parties. If none of these circumstances obtain, however, the evidence deriving from testimony, Hume stresses, may itself constitute a proof of the event testified: 'As the evidence, derived from witnesses and human testimony, is founded on past experience, so it ... is regarded as a proof or probability according as the conjunction between any particular kind of report and any kind of object has been found to be constant or variable' (Hume 1975: 112).

Even if the testimony has the nature of a proof, however, we may still reject it because proofs, unlike demonstrations, can be opposed by greater proofs. If the event attested is very unlikely, antecedently to the testimony, we will want more in the way of reliability from the witnesses than if it is a commonplace. Even though the character of the witness is impeccable, for all we know, and all the circumstances of the testimony favourable, the mere fact that what is attested is so implausible, says Hume, should set us on our guard:

> Suppose, for instance, that the fact which the teaching endeavours to establish, partake of the extraordinary or the marvellous: in that case the evidence, resulting from the testimony, admits of a diminution, greater or less, in proportion as the fact is more or less unusual. ... The very same principle of experience, which gives us a certain degree of assurance in the testimony of witnesses, gives us also, in this case, another degree of assurance against the fact ... from which contradiction there necessarily arises a ... mutual destruction of belief and authority.
>
> I should not believe such a story were it told me by Cato, was a proverbial saying in Rome. ... The incredibility of a fact it was allowed, might invalidate so great an authority.
>
> (Hume 1975: 113)

The more antecedently improbable the event reported, the more reliable the witness must be (the less likely to have made a false report) if he is to be believed, so that some reports would not be credible even if made by Cato. Consider a mundane illustration of this 'diminution principle' (so called by Earman 2000: 49). If you told me that travelling to London on a busy working day you did not see a single motorcycle on the road I would believe you – there are far fewer motorcycles than cars so your testimony is acceptable. But if instead you told me that you did not see a single car – only lorries and motorcycles – I would be very doubtful. I would not know what to think, but I would suspend judgement, and crucial to my eventual decision, if I came to one, would be my assessment of your reliability, determined by the probability of your giving this report if it were false, which latter would have to be very low, in relation to the probability of your giving it if it were true, for me to accept your testimony. The importance of this assessment is illustrated by a sort of case introduced by Richard Price (in Earman 2000) as a counter-example to what he takes to be Hume's diminution principle. (As interpreted here, following Owen [1987], the diminution principle is a platitude and a theorem of the probability calculus; Price interprets it as a stronger claim and interprets Hume as using it as his main weapon against miracles.) If a newspaper reports that in a million-ticket lottery, lottery number 79 won, I will believe this on the basis of the testimony – even though, antecedently it had only one chance in a million. It is the job of newspapers to be right about this sort of thing. But in this case it will be exceedingly unlikely that ticket number 79 would have been misreported as winning if any other number (say, 74,692) had won. And it will be enormously more likely that ticket 79 would have been reported as winning if it had in fact done so than if it had not. This is why, consistently with Hume's diminution principle, I accept the testimony of the newspaper, despite the immense prior improbability of the fact attested. The prior improbability is relevant, but can be set aside in this case, given the virtual certainty that ticket 79 would not have been reported as winning if some other number had. By contrast, in the cases he is concerned with – reports of marvels and miracles – Hume thinks, and argues in Part 2, the probability of misreport is quite high; for all sorts of psychological reasons people are quite likely to misreport that events of a striking, extraordinary, marvellous, miraculous and, particularly, religious character have occurred (this is why, reverting to the lottery example, we would be more suspicious if the newspaper reported that, say, number 666,666 had won).

Thus, as Hume explains, the possibility exists of a situation in which there is proof against proof: the testimony to an event constitutes a proof, since such testimony to such events by such witnesses has in all past cases been correct. But there is also a proof against the fact attested since a uniform experience counts against it. And in this case the diminution principle decrees that whatever proof wins out it must still be 'with a diminution of its force in proportion to that of its antagonist' (Hume 1975: 114).

But a miracle 'is a violation of the laws of nature, and as a firm and an unalterable experience has established the laws, the proof against a miracle is as entire as any argument from experience can possibly be imagined' (Hume 1975: 114).

A miracle then is, at the least, an event which conflicts with all past experience (in a footnote Hume gives what he calls a more accurate definition but nothing in his argument turns on it). So we are entitled, antecedently to encountering testimony, to be certain that the event never happened. It does not, however, follow that miracles are impossible, since by a 'law of nature' Hume does not mean a true universal generaliztion (much less a necessarily true one), but only a universal generalization to which no counter-instance has ever been encountered; it does not even follow that it must be irrational to believe in a miracle, since the testimonial proof may be stronger than the experiential proof against the miracle (one proof can be stronger than another if based on more instances or supported by analogous generalizations). But what does follow, Hume claims, is the general maxim already quoted: 'no testimony is sufficient to establish a miracle, unless the testimony be of such a kind, that its falsehood would be more miraculous than the fact it endeavours to establish' (Hume 1975: 115–16). In short, that we cannot accept a miracle on the basis of testimony unless we regard the falsehood of the testimony as more improbable (less probable) than the miracle attested. Or: we cannot accept a miracle on the basis of testimony unless we regard the miracle, given the testimony, as more probable than its non-occurrence.

This is where Part 1 ends, and it does so on an incontrovertible, indeed, near tautological, point. Hume has not argued that miracles are impossible, nor that belief in miracles is necessarily irrational, and he plainly believes neither of these things, since in Part 2 he describes a situation in which there would be decisive testimonial evidence in favour of a miracle. He imagines that all authors, in all languages, report that there was total darkness over the whole earth for eight days from January 1, 1600 and continues: 'it is evident that our present philosophers, instead of doubting the fact, ought to receive it as certain' (Hume 1975: 128).

The aim of Part 2 is first to convince us that no such situation has ever existed. It begins as follows: 'In the foregoing reasoning we have supposed, that the testimony, upon which a miracle is founded, may possibly amount to an entire proof. ... But it is easy to show that ... there never was a miraculous event established on so full an evidence' (Hume 1975: 116).

Hume gives four reasons for this claim:

First, there is not to be found in all history, any miracle attested by a sufficient number of men, of such unqualified good sense, education and learning, as to secure us against all delusion in themselves; of such undoubted integrity, as to place them beyond all suspicion of any design to deceive others; of such credit and reputation in the eyes of mankind, as to have a great deal to lose in case of their being detected in any falsehood; and at the same time, attesting facts, performed in such a public manner, and in so celebrated a part of the world, as to render the detection unavoidable. All of which circumstances are requisite to give us an assurance of the testimony of men.

(Hume 1975: 116)

'There is not to be found in all history', Hume claims. But how does he know? How could anyone know, granted the possibility both of miracles and of testimonial proofs thereof? Of course, that Hume does not know; nor does he care. His interest, as all his contemporary readers knew, was solely in the Christian revelation and its supposed certification by the miracle of the resurrection. His first contention is thus a direct challenge to orthodox Christian belief. In fact, Hume was writing in the wake of, and possibly in response to a celebrated eighteenth century debate in which Thomas Woolston had argued in his *Six Dissertations on the Miracles of Our Saviour* (1727–29) that the testimonial evidence for Christ's resurrection was unreliable. Thomas Sherlock replied on behalf of Christian orthodoxy in his *Tryal of the Witnesses of the Resurrection of Jesus* published in 1728. Hume is in effect announcing his rejection of Sherlock's response – though, very wisely, not explicitly (Woolston had ended his life in prison in 1733 after being convicted of criminal blasphemy).

In his first point he is thus in effect saying to Sherlock's defenders: 'Show me that the circumstances of the first witnesses to the Resurrection satisfied the conditions I have outlined on acceptable testimony to a miracle – or explain why these circumstances are not always necessary.'

Hume's second point is a plausible psychological thesis: that false testimony to miracles and marvels, unlike false testimony to such massively improbable but humdrum occurrences as the winning lottery ticket's number being 79, is very likely because 'the passion of surprise and wonder, arising from miracles ... gives a sensible tendency towards the belief of these events'. Moreover, additional considerations should make us even more sceptical of testimony to religious miracles,

> [I]f the spirit of religion joins itself to the love of wonder, there is an end of common sense. ... A religionist may be an enthusiast, and imagine he sees what has no reality: He may know his narrative false, and yet persevere in it, with the best intentions in the world, for the sake of promoting so holy a cause: ... vanity operates on him more powerfully than on the rest of mankind. ... His auditors ... commonly have not sufficient judgment to correct his evidence. ... Their credulity increases his impudence: And his impudence overpowers their credulity.
>
> (Hume 1975: 117)

Hume's third point is that tales of miracles arise first among ignorant and barbarous nations and 'grow thinner in every page as we advance nearer the enlightened ages' (Hume 1975: 119). This highlights the need for a believer in ancient miracles who rejects contemporary ones to tell a story to explain why the world has thus changed. For Hume himself, there is no problem: 'it is strange, a judicious reader is apt to say ... that such prodigious events never happen in our days. But it is nothing strange, I hope, that men should lie in all ages' (Hume 1975: 119–20).

Hume's fourth point is what has been called the 'contrary miracles argument':

> I may add as a fourth reason, which diminishes the authority of prodigies, that there is no testimony for any, even those which have not been expressly detected, that is not opposed by an infinite number of witnesses, so that not only the miracle destroys the credit of the testimony, but the testimony destroys itself.
>
> (Hume 1975: 121)

Hume's thought is that 'in matters of religion, whatever is different is contrary': each religion claims to be the sole true one and the only one with which genuine miracles are associated. Thus if we accept the miracles of one religion we must accept it as the true one, reject all others as false and conclude that all miracles reported by their followers are fake, no matter how difficult it is to impugn the testimony for the latter looked at in itself. Consequently, the testimony in favour of any miracle is opposed by 'an infinite number of witnesses'.

This argument is over-general, of course, since no polytheistic religion and not all monotheistic religions make such strong claims to exclusivity as Hume assumes, but it is appropriate for Hume to use it since the Biblical miracles were regarded by his eighteenth century theistic opponents as proofs of the exclusive revelation of Christianity – a religion whose believers are committed to 'believe in one God, the Father Almighty, Maker of heaven and earth, and of all things visible and invisible'.

Hume next introduces some entertaining tales of contemporary miracles, apparently accepting that the testimonies in support of them amount to proofs, but nonetheless rejecting them in what has seemed to many commentators to be a question-begging way: 'what have we to oppose to such a cloud of witnesses, but the absolute impossibility or miraculous nature of the events, which they relate? And this, surely, in the eyes of all reasonable people, will alone be regarded as sufficient refutation' (Hume 1975: 125).

It is hard not to acknowledge that Hume is being inconsistent here and allowing his anti-Christian prejudices to show through the pose of philosophical neutrality. He returns immediately, however, to his theme that 'no testimony for a miracle has in fact ever amounted to a probability, much less a proof' (Hume 1975: 115–16), and distinguishes this thesis from the less general but modally stronger thesis that 'no human testimony can have such force as to prove a miracle and make it a just foundation for a system of religion'.

The distinction is made by reference to the example of the eight days of darkness, which Hume then distinguishes from a similar secular miracle, whose possibility he rejects:

Suppose that all historians who treat of England, should agree that on the first of January 1600, Queen Elizabeth died: that before and after she was seen by her physicians and the whole court ... and that, after being interred a month, she again appeared [and] resumed the throne. [He goes on] I should not have the least inclination to believe so miraculous an event. ... The knavery and folly of men are such common phenomena that I should rather believe the most extraordinary events to arise from their concurrence than admit so signal a violation of the laws of nature.

(Hume 1975: 128)

The most obvious difference between the cases is the multiplicity of independent witnesses in the first case and the restriction of the reports in the second to 'all historians who treat of England'. As Hume says earlier: 'the wise lend a very academic faith to every report which favours the passion of the reporter: whether it magnifies his country, his family or himself' (Hume 1975: 125). However, this does not appear to be Hume's reason for distinguishing the cases. What this is emerges at the end of the discussion of the 'eight days of darkness'. Here Hume says that 'the decay, corruption and dissolution of nature, is an event rendered probable by so many analogies, that any phenomenon, which seems to have a tendency towards that catastrophe, comes within the reach of human testimony, if that testimony be very extensive and uniform' (Hume 1975: 128). Rightly or wrongly, Hume thinks that whereas there is a way of seeing an eight-days darkness as fitting in with, rather than contradicting, past experience, there is no similar way of seeing the resurrection of a dead woman as fitting in with past experience (which is perhaps why he refers to the putative resurrection not merely as 'a violation' but as 'so signal a violation' of the laws of nature).

At any rate, Hume now adds:

Should this new miracle be ascribed to any new system of religion men in all ages have been so imposed on by ridiculous stories that this very circumstance would be a full proof of a cheat. ... As the violations of truth are more common in the testimony concerning religious miracles, than in that concerning any other matter of fact ... this must ... make us form a general resolution never to lend any attention to it, with whatever specious pretence it may be covered.

(Hume 1975: 128–9)

Hume is here drawing attention again to the second of his four points and going as far as he dares to deny the credibility of the testimony of the resurrection. The psychological thesis upon which he rests his case is empirical, so cannot provide him with a demonstration that testimony to a miracle can never provide a rational foundation for a religion, but it can still constitute a proof. Hume clearly thinks it does and ends the section with the heavily ironical declaration:

> [W]e may conclude that the Christian Religion not only was at first attended with miracles, but even to this day cannot be believed by any reasonable person without one. Mere reason is insufficient to convince us of its veracity. And whoever is moved by Faith to assent to it, is conscious of a continuous miracle in his own person, which subverts all the principles of his understanding, and gives him a determination to believe what is most contrary to custom and experience.

(Hume 1975: 131)

Natural religion

Hume's critique of natural religion, the second possible foundation for rational belief in God, occurs in the section of the first *Enquiry* following the discussion of miracles and in its most sophisticated and detailed form in the posthumously published *Dialogues Concerning Natural Religion* (Hume 1998), on which Hume worked for many years, making the final additions in the year of his death.

The *Dialogues* has three speakers: Cleanthes, the advocate of an 'argument a posteriori', the argument from design; Demea, the advocate of an 'argument a priori', the cosmological argument; and Philo, the sceptic, who (as mentioned in the Introduction) puzzlingly appears to abandon all his sceptical scruples at the beginning of the final part and confesses a 'profound adoration to the divine Being, as he discovers himself to reason' (Hume 1998: 116). The dialogue between these speakers is narrated by Pamphilus, a pupil of Cleanthes, to his friend Hermippus. Pamphilus distributes honours at the end of the *Dialogues*, announcing that 'upon a serious review of the whole, I cannot but think that Philo's principles are more probable than Demea's, but that those of Cleanthes approach nearer to the truth' (Hume 1998: 130). It is this statement by Pamphilus, together with Philo's apparent reversal in the final part that has caused scholars to debate 'Who speaks for Hume?', despite the fact that it appears on the whole that Philo gets the better of the argument and certainly has the most to say.

Hume's likely model for the *Dialogues* was Cicero's *De Natura Deorum* (*Concerning the Nature of the Gods*, 1933), in which a dialogue between Velleius, an Epicurean, Balbus, a Stoic, and Cotta, an Academic Sceptic, and critic of the others, is reported by a young Cicero. Cicero was himself a member of the Academic School and Cotta was one of his best friends. The dialogue ends, however, in a way that clearly provides the model for Hume's ending to his *Dialogues*, with Cicero surprisingly endorsing the views of the Stoic Balbus – one indication that the endorsement by Pamphilus of Cleanthes' position should not be relied upon as a pointer to Hume's own position. Cotta and Cicero himself had been taught by Philo of Larissa, one of the sceptical heads of the New Academy and the Stoic Cleanthes is one of the authorities of Cicero's Stoic Balbus. It is reasonable to assume that Hume would have expected his educated readers to be aware of these facts, to pick up the significance of the names, to recognize the identification Hume was therefore implying of himself as author with the Academic Cicero, and to take the final assessment of Pamphilus (who is anyway described as a pupil of Cleanthes) with a considerable pinch of salt.

But the strongest reason for receiving Pamphilus' assessment with reservation is simply that the *Dialogues* as a whole and Philo's contribution in particular, is a devastating critique of natural religion and specifically of the argument from design. As Bernard Williams once wrote: 'Sir Leslie Stephen said that the *Dialogues* was the first sustained philosophical criticism of the Argument from Design. I do not know for certain whether this is true; what is certain is that, in a slightly different sense, it is the last – after it there did not need to be another' (Williams 1963: 84–5). If Hume really thought that Cleanthes got the better of the debate he simply failed to see the force of his own arguments.

The *Dialogues* is divided into twelve parts, the first is introductory, the second to the eighth concern the argument from design, the ninth provides a critique, through Cleanthes' mouth, of the Cosmological Argument, ten and eleven are concerned with the Problem of Evil and in the final part Hume makes Philo declare his adoration of the divine Being and provides commentators with the discussion of his intentions which has been hotly debated ever since.

Given the length and complexity of the arguments of the *Dialogues* we must be selective. I shall outline only one thread of argument against the argument from design, the strongest and most straightforward; say something about Hume's attitude to the problem of evil; and look at some features of the enigmatic final section, to see how little, in fact, Philo and Hume commit themselves to in the end.

The argument from design, as Hume understands it, is an argument from analogy. In Cleanthes' words:

> Contemplate the whole and every part of it. You will find it to be one great machine, subdivided into an infinite number of lesser machines. ... All these various machines ... are adjusted to each other with an accuracy, which ravishes with admiration all men, who have ever contemplated them. The curious adapting of means to ends, throughout all nature, resembles exactly, though it much exceeds, the productions of human contrivance. ... Since therefore the effects resemble each other, we are led to infer, by all the rules of analogy, that the causes also resemble; and that the Author of Nature is somewhat similar to the mind of man. ... By this argument a posteriori, and by this argument alone, do we prove at once the existence of a Deity and his similarity to human mind and intelligence.
>
> (Hume 1998: 45)

The argument from design is an argument a posteriori, since 'Order, arrangement, or the adjustment of final causes is not, of itself, any proof of design; but only so far as it has been experienced to proceed from that principle' (Hume 1998: 48).

Philo's strongest objection to the design argument, only fully developed in Part VII, is that the assumption on which the whole argument rests, that order, arrangement and the adjustment of final causes 'proceed from that principle', turns out, when we do consult experience, to be unsupported by it. Order and arrangement of final causes do indeed, in some cases, observably arise from design, but in other cases, and a greater number, they observably arise from other principles. Since it is experience only on which we can rely we therefore cannot infer that ultimately all order must arise from design.

Philo introduces this argument after suggesting, in Part VI, that the comparison of the world to an animal is at least as apt as its comparison to a machine. Cleanthes does not resist this suggestion strongly, but only suggests that the comparison to a vegetable is still more apt (Hume 1998: 74). The reason that Cleanthes cannot simply reject these analogies is that resemblance is symmetrical. So if the world as a whole and all its parts resemble human artefacts, human artefacts and the world as a whole equally resemble the other parts of the world, animal and vegetable. This is all that Philo's subsequent argument in Part VII needs, although his exposition starts from the assumption, not challenged by Cleanthes, that the world as a whole is more similar to an animal or vegetable than to a human artefact: 'If the universe bears a greater likeness to animal bodies and to vegetables, than to works of human art, it is more probable that its cause resembles the cause of the former than that of the latter' (Hume 1998: 78).

Spelling this out for Demea, who helpfully says that he does not understand it in the 'concise manner' expounded, Philo first emphasizes again that 'since no question of fact can be proved otherwise than by experience', the existence of a Deity can have no other sort of proof (Hume 1998: 78). This is the crucial point for him. Examining the world without preconceptions we see that in putting forward the argument from design Cleanthes is taking 'the operation of one small part of nature, to wit man, upon another small part, to wit, that inanimate matter lying within his reach' as the rule by which to judge of the whole; but experience shows that 'there are other parts of the universe' upon which we can equally well base a hypothesis about its origin (Hume 1998: 78). The world resembles animals and plants as much as it does a watch or a knitting loom, but the causes of these, we know from experience, are not the activities of intelligent designers.

Demea's role throughout Part VII is to put questions that allow Philo to emphasize the need for the champion of the argument from design to defend his assumptions from experience. Thus Demea's next question is: 'But how is it conceivable that the world can arise from anything similar to vegetation or germination?'

But, of course, for Hume, anything can arise from anything, so Philo offers an illustration: 'in a like manner as a tree sheds its leaves into the neighbouring fields and produces other trees; so the great vegetable, the world ... produces within itself other seeds, which being scattered into the surrounding chaos vegetate into new worlds'. This is not meant as a serious suggestion, but only as a hypothesis, as intelligible as any if an answer is demanded. Philo's position remains firmly sceptical, as the next exchange with Demea makes clear:

I understand you, says Demea: But what wild arbitrary suppositions are these? What data have you for such extraordinary conclusions? ... is the slight imaginary resemblance of the world to a vegetable or an animal sufficient to establish the same inference with regard to both? Objects, which are in general so widely different, ought they to be the standard for each other?

Right [cries Philo]. This is the topic on which I have all along insisted. I have still asserted that we have no data to establish any system of cosmogony. Our experience, ... can afford us no probable conjecture concerning the whole of things. But if we must needs fix on some hypothesis ... [is] there any other rule than the greater similarity of the objects compared? And does not a plant or an animal ... bear a stronger resemblance to the world than does any artificial machine?

(Hume 1998: 79)

Demea's next question reveals that he still has not seen Philo's point: he asks him to explain the operations of vegetation and generation – as if the justification for Philo's inference requires such an explanation.

Philo responds, 'when I see an animal, I infer that it sprang from generation, and that with as great certainty as you conclude a house to have been reared by design'. He goes on:

> These words, generation, reason mark only certain powers and energies in nature, whose effects are known, but whose essence is incomprehensible; and one of these principles, more than the other has no privilege for being the standard for the whole of nature ... In this little corner of the world alone, there are four principles, reason, instinct, generation, and vegetation, which are similar to each other and are the causes of similar effects. ... Any one of these ... principles ... may afford us theory, by which to judge of the origin of the world; ... it is a palpable and egregious partiality, to confine our view ... to that principle on which our own minds operate. ... The effects of these principles are all known from experience. But the principles themselves, and their manner of operation, are totally unknown: Nor is it less intelligible, or less conformable to experience to say that the world arose by vegetation ... than to say that it arose from a divine reason or contrivance.
>
> (Hume 1998: 80)

We do not have to know how a principle operates in order legitimately to suppose that it does operate, and the 'essence' of reason, its mechanism of operation, is no more known than the 'essence' of such powers as generation and vegetation.

This is Philo's argument complete. But Hume allows Demea one more question in order to make clear again the limitations imposed on the argument from design by its dependence on experience.

Demea objects: 'If the world had a vegetative quality and could sow the seeds of new worlds ... whence could arise so wonderful a faculty but from design? Or how could order spring from anything which perceives not the order which it bestows' (Hume 1998: 80–81).

To this protest Philo's reply comes in two parts. First, he points out that order arises in this way all the time: 'A tree bestows order ... on that tree which springs from it, an animal ... on its offspring, a bird on its nest', and does so far more frequently than order arises from design.

Of course, the defender of Demea will argue that this is not to the point: acorns grow into oaks, and acorns are not intelligent, but ultimately the order displayed by the oak and the causal sequence from which it arises, must proceed from something which is 'aware of the order which it bestows'.

It is this thought that the second part of Philo's reply targets:

> To say that all this order in animals and vegetables proceeds ultimately from design is begging the question; nor can that great point be ascertained but by proving a priori both that order is, from its nature, inseparably attached to thought, and that it never can, of itself ... belong to matter.
>
> (Hume 1998: 81)

Moreover, if arguments a priori are set aside, and it is agreed that the two hypotheses of design and generation are equally intelligible, then Hume points out that what little relevant experience we have favours the latter, for we see every day intelligence developing in living organisms, and never in anything else, and we have no experience of living organisms created by design.

This response to the design argument turns, in the end, on the simple point that the totality of our experience of the world must be the basis of any inference to its cause, not just some small part of it that happens to fit in with our argumentative purposes. The same point is the burden of Hume's discussion of the problem of evil in Parts X and XI of the *Dialogues*. He allows that the evil that exists in the world is consistent with the hypothesis of a benevolent designer (given our ignorance we cannot know what reasons God might have for allowing evil), but insists that we have no grounds to infer from the world as a whole, with its mix of good and evil, to its creation by such a designer:

> Is the world considered in general, and as it appears to us in this life, different from what a man ... would, beforehand, expect from a very powerful, wise and benevolent Diety? It must be a strange prejudice to assert the contrary. And from thence I conclude, that, however consistent the world may be, allowing certain suppositions and conjectures, with the idea of such a Deity, it can never afford us an inference concerning his existence. The consistence is not absolutely denied, only the inference.
>
> (Hume 1998: 107)

Philo's (and Hume's) bleak view of the world is given eloquent expression:

> Look round this universe ... inspect a little more narrowly these living existences. ... How hostile and destructive to each other! How insufficient all of them for their own happiness! How contemptible or odious to the spectator! The whole presents nothing but the idea of a blind nature, impregnated by a great vivifying principle, and pouring forth from her lap, without discernment or parental care, her maimed and abortive children.
>
> (Hume 1998: 113)

Hume sums up by outlining the possibilities and assigning probabilities:

> There may four hypotheses be found concerning the first cause of the universe: that they are endowed with perfect goodness, that they have perfect malice, that they are opposite and have both goodness and malice, that they have neither goodness nor malice. Mixed phenomena can never prove the two former unmixed principles. And the uniformity and steadiness of general laws seem to oppose the third. The fourth therefore seems by far the most probable.
>
> (Hume 1998: 114)

Here Hume, or Philo, goes further than his sceptical stance should allow: if the fourth hypothesis is most probable, then the first, being incompatible with it, must be on balance improbable (less that 50 per cent probable) and to be rejected. But Hume does not need to go so far to reject the inference to a benevolent deity – all he needs is that the fourth hypothesis is at least as probable as the first. It seems likely that here, for once, the man has got the better of the philosopher.

Finally, we can turn to the last part of the *Dialogues* and Philo's surprising apparent reversal.

The context is the following. Demea, at last seeing behind Philo's pretence of agreement with him in opposition to Cleanthes cries out: 'I joined in alliance with you, in order to ... refute the principles of Cleanthes. But I now find you running into all the topics of the greatest libertines and infidels. ... Are you secretly, then, a more dangerous enemy than Cleanthes himself?' (Hume 1998: 114–15).

This is Demea's last word. Philo does not answer. But Cleanthes replies for him: 'Are you so late in perceiving it? ... your friend Philo, from the beginning has been amusing himself at both our expence' (Hume 1998: 115).

Part XI finishes with Pamphilus informing us that 'Demea did not at all relish the latter part of the discourse, and he took occasion soon after, ... to leave the company' (Hume 1998: 115).

Thus Part XII begins after an exchange of harsh words and a display of ill feeling. Cleanthes admonishes Philo: 'Our friend will have little inclination to revive this topic ... while you are in company ... your spirit of controversy ... carries you to strange lengths ... and there is nothing so sacred and venerable you spare on that occasion' (Hume 1998: 117).

Philo's fulsome confession of his 'adoration to the divine Being' follows:

> [N]o one pays more attention to the divine Being, as he discovers himself to reason, in ... nature. A purpose, an intention, a design strikes everywhere the most careless, the most stupid thinker, and no man can be so hardened in absurd systems as at all times to reject it. ... All the sciences almost lead us insensibly to acknowledge a first intelligent Author.
>
> (Hume 1998: 117)

It is reasonable to see this in part as an attempt to restore amicable relations, but this does not seem sufficient to explain the emphatic tone of Philo's reversal, which has left commentators puzzled about Hume's intentions. Some have taken him to be indicating here an endorsement of, or at least an appreciation of the strength of, the 'irregular' form of the argument from design Cleanthes gives in Part III, after which Philo is silent and described by Pamphilus as 'embarrassed'.

However this may be, that Philo's reversal is less sincere than it seems quickly becomes apparent. Cleanthes, taking Philo now to be in agreement with him and forgetting all the criticisms made of it, repeats his advocacy of the 'principle of theism' and his rejection of scepticism:

> [T]he comparison of the universe to a machine ... is so obvious and natural, and justified by so many instances of order and design in nature, that it must immediately strike all unprejudiced apprehensions, and procure universal approbation ... suspense of judgment]... is in itself unsatisfactory ... it can never be steadily maintained ... I think it absolutely impossible to maintain or defend.
>
> (Hume 1998: 118)

Philo agrees about the impossibility of suspense of judgment, but his reason reveals the limited extent of his reversal. The theist and the atheist are not in genuine disagreement; their controversy is a 'dispute of words':

> The works of nature bear a great analogy to the productions of art ... we ought to infer, if we argue at all concerning them, their causes have a proportional analogy ... as there are also considerable differences, we have reason to suppose a proportional difference in the causes. ... Here then the existence of a Deity is plainly ascertained by reason ... whether, on account of the analogies, we can properly call him a mind or intelligence, notwithstanding the vast difference between him and human minds: What is this but a mere verbal controversy?
>
> (Hume 1998: 119)

The point is made so that it cannot be missed in material added, significantly, in the final revision of the *Dialogues* in the year of Hume's death:

> I ask the theist, if he does not allow, that there is a great and immeasurable, because incomprehensible, difference between the human and the divine mind: the more pious he is the more readily he will assent ..., and the more will he be disposed to magnify the difference ... I turn next to the atheist, who, I assert, is only nominally so ... and I ask him, whether, from the coherence and apparent sympathy in all the parts of this world, there be not a certain degree of analogy among all the operations of nature, ... whether the rotting of a turnip, the generation of an animal, and the structure of human thought be not energies that probably have some remote analogy to each other. It is impossible he can deny it. ... I push him still

further ..., and I ask him, if it be not probable, that the principle which first arranged, and still maintains, order in this universe, bears also some remote inconceivable analogy to the other operations of nature, and among the rest to the economy of human mind and thought. However reluctant, he must give his assent. Where then, I cry to both of these antagonists, is the subject of your dispute? The theist allows that the original intelligence is very different from human reason: the atheist allows that the original principle of order bears some remote analogy to it. Will you quarrel, Gentlemen, about the degree, and enter into a controversy, which admits not of any precise meaning, nor consequently of any determination?

(Hume 1998: 120)

There are four things to note about this added material. First, Hume recalls the reader's attention to the hypotheses of Parts VI and VII and the comparisons of the universe to a vegetable and an animal. Second, he does so using an example, the rotting turnip, which could not have been more carefully calculated to irritate the-istic sensibility. Third, he uses the word 'principle', recalling the four principles of Part VII: reason, instinct, generation and vegeta-tion. Fourth, he repeatedly formulates what he is suggesting is the common intelligible content of the position of the atheist and the theist, when stated so as to be undeniable by the atheist, using the expression 'some remote analogy' (three times in four sentences).

When he states in the final paragraph of Philo's last speech, also added in the final revision of 1776, the italicized proposition to which he suggests 'some people' think the whole of natural the-ology resolves, he uses the expression again 'the cause, or causes, of order in the universe probably bear some remote analogy to human intelligence' (Hume 1998: 129).

He does not add here, as he does in the first of the 1776 additions, 'and to the other operations of nature', but he hopes his reader will see the point. At the beginning of the *Dialogues*, in Part II, Philo affirms: 'the question can never be concerning the being, but only the nature of the Deity. The former truth ... is unquestionable and self-evident. Nothing exists without a cause, and the original cause of this universe (whatever it be) we call God' (Hume 1998: 44).

Philo and Hume end where they begin.

Bibliography

Anscombe, G. E. M. (1981) *The Collected Philosophy Papers. Volume Two: Metaphysics and the Philosophy of Mind*, Minneapolis, MN: University of Minnesota Press.

Baier, A. (1991) *A Progress of Sentiments: Reflections on Hume's 'Treatise'*, Cambridge, MA: Harvard University Press.

Basson, A. H. (1958) *David Hume*, Middlesex: Penguin Books.

Beauchamp, T. and Rosenberg, A. (1981) *Hume and the Problem of Causation*, Oxford: Oxford University Press.

Bennett, J. (1971) *Locke, Berkeley and Hume*, Oxford: Clarendon Press.

Bennett, J. (2001) *Learning from Six Philosophers*, vol. 2, Oxford: Clarendon Press.

Berkeley, G. (1949) *The Works of George Berkeley*, vol. II, eds A. A. Luce and T. E. Jessop, London: Thomas Nelson and Sons Limited.

Boswell, J. (1947) 'Interview with Hume, 7 July 1776', in Norman Kemp Smith's edition of the *Dialogues*, Indianapolis, IN: Bobbs-Merrill, 76–9.

Broad, C. D. (1916–17) 'Hume's Theory of the Credibility of Miracles', *Proceedings of the Aristotelian Society* 17:77–94.

Broad, C. D. (1962) *The Mind and Its Place in Nature*, London: Routledge and Kegan Paul.

Broughton, J. (1983) 'Causal inferences', *Pacific Philosophical Quarterly* 64:3–18.

Butler, J. (1736) 'Of personal identity', *First dissertation to The Analogy of Religion*, reprinted in A. Flew (1964) *Body, Mind and Death*, New York: Macmillan; J. Perry (ed.) (1975) *Personal Identity*, Berkeley and Los Angeles, CA: University of California Press.

Chisholm, R. M. (1976) *Person and Object*, London: Allen and Unwin.

Cicero, M. (1933) *Cicero*, vol. 19, trans. R. H. Rackham, Cambridge, MA: Harvard University Press.

Connon, R. W. (1979) 'The naturalism of Hume revisited', in *McGill Hume Studies*, San Diego, CA: Austin Hill Press, 121–45.

Cook, J. (1968) 'Hume's scepticism with regard to the senses', *American Philosophical Quarterly* 5:1–17.

Descartes, R. (1984) *The Philosophical Writings of Descartes*, vol. 2, ed. and trans. J. Cottingham, R. Stoothoff, and D. Murdoch, Cambridge: Cambridge University Press.

Earman J. (2000) *Hume's Abject Failure: The Argument Against Miracles*, Oxford: Oxford University Press.

Flew, A. (1961) *Hume's Philosophy Of Belief*, London: Routledge and Kegan Paul.

Flew, A. (1986) *Hume: Philosopher of Moral Science*, Oxford: Blackwell.

Fogelin, R. (1985) *Hume's Skepticism in the Treatise of Human Nature*, London: Routledge and Kegan Paul.

Fogelin, R. (1992) *Philosophical Interpretations*, Oxford: Oxford University Press.

Fogelin, J. (2003) *A Defense of Hume on Miracles*, Princeton, NJ: Princeton University Press.

Garrett, D. (1981) 'Hume's self doubts about personal identity', *Philosophical Review* 90:337–58.

Garrett, D. (1997) *Cognition and Commitment in Hume's Philosophy*, Oxford: Oxford University Press.

Garrett, D. (2005) 'Hume, David (1711–76)', in the *Routledge Encyclopedia of Philosophy Online*, London: Routledge.

Goodman, N. (1955) *Fact, Fiction and Forecast*, Cambridge, MA: Harvard University Press.

Hobbes, T. (1994) *The English Works of Thomas Hobbes*, vol. 1, ed. Sir William Molesworth, London: John Bohn, 1839. Reprinted London: Routlege/Thoemmes Press.

Hume, D. (1948) *Moral and Political Philosophy*, ed. D. Aitken, New York: Hafner Publishing Company.

Hume, D. (1975) *Enquiries Concerning Human Understanding and Concerning the Principles of Morals*, 3rd edn. Ed. L. A. Selby-Bigge and P. H. Nidditch, Oxford: Oxford University Press.

Hume, D. (1978) *A Treatise of Human Nature*, 2nd edn. ed. L. A. Selby-Bigge, and P. H. Nidditch, Oxford: Oxford University Press.

Hume, D. (1993a) 'A kind of history of my life', in D. F. Norton (ed.) *The Cambridge Companion to Hume*, Cambridge: Cambridge University Press.

Hume, D. (1993b) 'My own life', in D. F. Norton (ed.) *The Cambridge Companion to Hume*, Cambridge: Cambridge University Press.

Hume, D. (1998) *Dialogues and Natural History of Religion*, (ed.) J. A. Gaskin, Oxford: Oxford University Press.

Kant, I (1977) *Prolegomena to Any Future Metaphysics*, Indianapolis, IN: Hackett Publishing Company.

Kemp Smith, N. (1941) *The Philosophy of David Hume*, London: Macmillan.

Kripke S. (1980) *Naming and Necessity*, revised edn., Oxford: Blackwell.

Leibniz, G. W. (1981) *New Essays on Human Understanding*, trans. and ed. P. Remnant and J. Bennett, Cambridge: Cambridge University Press.

Lewis, C. S. (1947) *Miracles*, London: G Bles.

Lewis, D. (1983) 'New work for a theory of universals', *Australasian Journal of Philosophy* 61:343–79.

Lewis, D. (1984) 'Putnam's Paradox', *Australasian Journal of Philosophy* 62:221–36.

Locke, J. (1961) *An Essay Concerning Human Understanding*, ed. J. Yolton, London: Dent.

Loeb, L. (1991) 'Stability, justification and Hume's propensity to ascribe identity to related objects', *Philosophical Studies* 19:237–69.

Loeb, L. (1995a) 'Hume on stability justification and unphilosophical probability', *Journal of the History of Philosophy* 33:101–31.

Loeb, L. (1995b) 'Instability and uneasiness in Hume's theories of belief and justification', *British Journal of the History of Philosophy* 3, 2:301–29.

Loeb, L. (2002) *Stability and Justification in Hume's Treatise*, New York: Oxford University Press.

Mackie, J. (1974) *The Cement of the Universe: A Study of Causation*, Oxford: Oxford University Press.

Mackie, J. (1980) *Hume's Moral Theory*, London: Routledge.

Malebranche, N. (1700) *Father Malebranche: His Search after Truth, to which is Added the Treatise of Nature and Grace*, London.

Malebranche, N. (1968) *Oeuvres completes*, ed. Andre Robinet, 20 vols.

Malebranche, N. (1980) *The Search after Truth*, trans. T. M. Lennon and P. J. Olscamp, with a commentary by T. M. Lennon, Columbus, OH: Ohio State University Press.

BIBLIOGRAPHY

McCracken, C. J. (1983) *Malebranche and British Philosophy*, Oxford: Clarendon Press.

Mossner, C. E. (1948) 'Hume's Early Memoranda, 1729–1740: The Complete Text', *Journal of the History of Ideas* 9:492–518.

Mossner, C. E. (1954) *The Life of David Hume*, Austin, TX: University of Texas Press.

Norton, D. F. (ed.) (1993) *The Cambridge Companion to Hume*, Cambridge: Cambridge University Press.

Owen. D. (1987) 'Hume versus Price on Miracles and Prior Probabilities: Testimony and the Bayesian Calculation', *Philsophical Quarterly* 37:187–202.

Owen, D. (1999) *Hume's Reason*, Oxford: Oxford University Press.

Parfit, D. (1986) *Reason and Persons*, Oxford: Clarendon Press.

Penelhum, T. (1955) 'Hume on personal identity', *Philosophical Review* 64:571–89.

Pike, N. (1967) 'Hume's bundle theory of the self: a limited defence', *American Philosophical Quarterly* 4:159–65.

Popkin, R. H. (1964) 'So, Hume did read Berkeley', *Journal of Philosophy* 61:774–5.

Raphael, D. D. (ed.) (1991) *British Moralists 1650–1800*, Indianapolis, IN: Hackett Publishing Company.

Reid, T. (1941) *Essays on the Intellectual Powers of Man*, ed. A. D. Woozley, London: Macmillan.

Russell, B. (1912) *The Problems of Philosophy*, London: Williams and Norgate; New York: Henry Holt and Company.

Scruton, R. (1995) *A Short History of Modern Philosophy*, London: Routledge.

Sextus Empiricus (1933–49) *Sextus Empiricus with an English Translation*, trans. by R. G. Bury, 4 vols, Cambridge, MA: Harvard University Press, London: Heinnemann. *Outlines of Pyrrhonism* referred to as 'PH'.

Sherlock, T. (1728) *Tryal of the Witnesses of the Resurrection of Jesus*, London: J. Roberts.

Shoemaker, S. (1986) 'Introspection and the self', *Midwest Studies in Philosophy* 10:101–20.

Shoemaker, S. (1994) 'Self knowledge and inner sense', *Philosophy and Phenomenological Research*, 54:249–315.

Spinoza, B. (1949) *Ethics*, ed. J. Guttman, New York: Hafner Publishing Company Inc.

Stove, D. C. (1965) 'Hume, probability and induction', *Philosophical Review* 74:160–77.

Stove, D. C. (1973) *Probability and Hume's Inductive Scepticism*, Oxford: Clarendon Press.

Strawson. G. (1989) *The Secret Connexion: Causation, Realism and David Hume*, Oxford: Clarendon Press.

Stroud, B. (1977) *Hume*, London: Routledge and Kegan Paul.

Williams, B. A. O. (1963) 'Hume on Religion', in *David Hume: A Symposium*, ed. D. F. Pears, London: Macmillan and Co. Ltd.

Wittgenstein, L. (1968) *Philosophical Investigations*, trans. G. E. M. Anscombe, Oxford: Blackwell.

Woolston, T. (1727–29) *Six Discourses on the Miracles of our Savior*, London. Reprinted by Garland Publishing, New York, 1979.

Wright, J. (1983) *The Sceptical Realism of David Hume*, Manchester: Manchester University Press.

Yolton, J. (1970) *Locke and the Compass of Human Understanding*, Cambridge: Cambridge University Press.

Index

209